SO GOOD Richard Blais

100 RECIPES FROM MY KITCHEN TO YOURS

with Mary Goodbody
Photography by Evan Sung

HOUGHTON MIFFLIN HARCOURT
BOSTON NEW YORK 2017

Library of Congress Cataloging-in-Publication Data is available.

ISBN 978-0-544-66331-2 (hardcover);

978-0-544-66309-1 (ebook)

Design by Gary Tooth/Empire Design Studio

Printed in China

C&C 10 9 8 7 6 5 4 3 2 1

FOR MY FAMILY:
Jazmin Blais, Riley Blais, and Embry Blais.
Without you, there would be nothing.

CON-TENTS

ACKNOWLEDGMENTS

Thanks to those who helped make this book: Justin Schwartz, Mary Goodbody, Evan Sung, Kira Corbin, Michael Psaltis, Kate Wagoner, Scarlett Brida, and the numerous cooks who touched and cooked beautiful food for this book.

For those who hold down the forts . . . er . . . restaurants: Brad Chance, Anthony Wells, Jon Sloan, Dan Pena, Mike Rosen, and the more than numerous cooks and employees who work so hard and with passion for our restaurants and eating establishments.

And for those who make the magic happen in this boy's life: Cameron Molinaro, Lisa Shotland, and Adam Nettler.

I'm a restaurant chef, but I love to cook at home. I am totally comfortable in my home kitchen and, more to the point, I have a wife and two young kids who need to eat and who like to eat. Hey, lucky me!

So here's a collection of recipes that work at home and that you'll want to prepare time and again. They aren't restaurant dishes with complicated cooking instructions and tons of garnishes. They don't require esoteric ingredients that could break the bank. I hope they're appealing and grab your interest. They have all earned their place in my kitchen arsenal.

Sure, because I'm who I am—a little cr-a-zy in the kitchen—a handful might be considered "out there." But why not? Some home cooks want a challenge. Maybe not every day, but now and then. And so, as you leaf through these pages, you'll see a recipe for pigs' feet . . . and one that calls for a lamb's head . . . and another that requires caul fat . . . and one for oxtail. . . . No worries! This is not a test. You are not obligated to try every recipe in the book. But because I always suggest familiar ingredients to replace the more unusual, I hope you won't skip them altogether!

Let's face it. Most of my recipes are pretty mainstream without—I hope!—being trite or boring. How about barbecued shrimp or pot roast? Or spaghetti with pesto, chicken with garlic and rosemary, or the juiciest burger you've ever tasted? (Want that recipe *right now*? Turn to page 154 for my Juicy Lucy.)

CURIOUSER AND CURIOUSER

I'm a curious cook. When I hear about a new or revived cooking technique, I'm first in line to buy any necessary equipment or ingredients. This is why I have the reputation for being a little wild, using liquid nitrogen in the kitchen and championing the sous vide method. I don't mind this rep, and while I know full well some folks aren't into these kinds of things, for those of us who are, they can be loads of fun and produce some really amazing results. But again, don't freak out. Whenever I heft the liquid nitrogen canister, I also supply more traditional cooking instructions that result in similar outcomes.

My curiosity extends to traditional cooking techniques and dishes, too. I love to explore the cuisines of various regions and countries. In *So Good*, I've developed recipes with deep Southern roots (fried chicken, buttermilk biscuits, fried pickles, and ham hocks with mustard greens), as well as others that owe a sweeping bow to Asia (a Hong Kong bowl, ramen noodles, and pork with pineapple fried rice). You'll find recipes here with their roots in Europe and the Middle East, as well as many others that are as American as apple pie.

Happily, this is how we cook nowadays. We grab an idea here, an ingredient there, a technique elsewhere, and put them all together to come up with truly crave-worthy dishes. Our grandparents wouldn't recognize the American kitchen these days, but I wager they'd love the food!

RESTAURANTS AND TV

I love my restaurants, which are in Atlanta, Birmingham, Nashville, and San Diego. The three in the South are Flip Burger Boutiques; I've always loved burgers! In California I have Juniper and Ivy, a more refined place that I like to say has "a left coast edge," and the Crack Shack. Crack Shack is my latest venture and, if I do say so, is pretty cool. We serve breakfast, lunch, and dinner with dishes centered around chicken and eggs. Wear shorts; bring an appetite.

As if these don't keep me busy enough, I also run around the country shooting various TV shows. My most recent gig is with *MasterChef* and *MasterChef Junior* on Fox, but readers might also know me from *Top Chef*, *Top Chef All-Stars*, *Iron Chef America*, and *Chopped All-Stars*. I've judged episodes of *Guy's Grocery Games* and *Cutthroat Kitchen*, and host *Burger Lab*, *Cook Your A$$ Off*, and *Man vs. Master* currently.

Writing this down makes me tired. I can't lie. But it also exhilarates me because I *love* the energy and excitement that so many people—pros and amateurs—share when it comes to food. We all eat, and many of us cook. It's how we show our love, get through bad times, and celebrate holidays and family milestones. And for so many of us, it's an outlet for our creativity.

LONG ISLAND DAYS

I grew up in suburban Long Island. Geographically I wasn't far from Manhattan, but I might as well have lived in Anywhere, USA. In other words, the tiny hamlet of Uniondale wasn't far from the city, but my childhood was, I suspect, very like that of any kid who lived in a working class suburb. We knew the great urban metropolis was down the road, but my friends and I didn't pay much attention to it.

The food of my childhood was fairly ordinary, too. I loved holidays and the special occasions when we ate in a restaurant—I came to adore the old-school shrimp cocktails my parents let me order. My first job was at McDonald's, which is where I realized I actually liked cooking for others. I like to say I was the *poissonier* there, since I held down the fish filet station.

I am not going to claim my stint under the Golden Arches had anything to do with my decision to go to cooking school, but off I went. After graduating from the Culinary Institute of America, I looked around for the most stimulating restaurants I could find and went on to train further at the French Laundry and Chez Panisse, both in Northern California; Daniel, in New York; and El Bulli, in Spain.

WELCOME TO MY KITCHEN

How, you ask, do I find time to cook for my wife and two daughters, as I claimed I do when I began writing this book? It's tough, but we manage. I try to be home on weekends, when I make big cauldrons of soup, full-bodied braises, and robust pasta dishes. The kids love this kind of food, as do my wife, Jazmin, and I. They fill the house with homey and comforting aromas, the kind that signal that whatever is going on elsewhere, for the time being all is well *chez* Blais. We pull our chairs up to the kitchen table and dig in.

I hope with *So Good* in hand, you and yours will do the same. Happy cooking and eating!

STARTERS

Starters, apps, small plates, snacks . . . however you want to define them, these are can-be (could-be?) meals. Sure, if you're in the mood for a fancy dinner party, any one of these will inaugurate the meal in grand style. On the other hand, many of the recipes in this chapter are a slice of bread away from a sandwich. I call that lunch.

I love coming up with these—to root around in the refrigerator for bits and pieces of leftovers, condiments, pungent pastes, and jarred luxuries to create small culinary treasures. Whether I am in a professional kitchen or a customer in a restaurant, these, and sides, are the first dishes I think about. You, too? Read on!

When I first developed this recipe, I was relying on the Cryovac food-vacuum system and so called the salmon "almost-cured." If you don't use this system but decide to cure the fish the old-fashioned way, plan to prepare it a few days before serving. It's super easy but takes time, and you might need to add more salt to cover the fish completely. Regardless of how you cure it, be sure to rinse the salmon very well under cool water. Get rid of that salt!

I love that a softened compound butter is essential to this recipe. When's the last time you saw that? Probably never. Or perhaps as recently as this morning, if you opted for butter over cream cheese on your bagel! And finally, if you have a wild celery plant growing nearby, as I do, a few of its blossoms make a great visual addition.

ALMOST-CURED SALMON
WITH HORSERADISH

In a small mixing bowl, stir together the salt, sugar, 2 tablespoons of the dill, the vodka (if using), 2 tablespoons of the lemon zest, and 1 tablespoon of the horseradish.

Lay the salmon on a large sheet of plastic wrap. Sprinkle the salt mixture over the fillet, covering it entirely. If necessary, add a little more salt. Wrap the salmon in the plastic wrap and then wrap in a layer of aluminum foil.

Transfer the wrapped salmon to a shallow dish and set a smaller dish on top of it. Weight the fish by setting a couple of heavy cans on the smaller dish. Refrigerate for at least 24 hours and up to 3 days. The longer end of the scale is better!

Alternatively, put the seasoned salmon in a Cryovac bag. Seal according to the manufacturer's instructions and set aside for at least 1 hour. (An hour in Cryovac is the equivalent of about 12 hours in the refrigerator.)

Preheat the oven to 350°F.

Spread the pumpernickel cubes on a baking sheet and bake for 8 to 10 minutes, until crisp, turning the croutons once during toasting. If you prefer, you can toast the croutons in a skillet on top of the stove in a little melted butter.

In a sauté pan, heat the olive oil over medium-high heat. Add the garlic and onions and cook, stirring and taking care not to burn the garlic, until the onions are translucent and have released their juices, 2 to 3 minutes. Stir in the remaining 1 tablespoon horseradish and the parsley. Let cool to room temperature. When cool, combine the onion mixture with the butter and mash with a fork or use a spoon to mix well. Set aside at room temperature to soften a little more.

Remove the salmon from the wrapping or the Cryovac bag and rinse well under cool running water; pat dry. Slice the fish into thin pieces. Cover and refrigerate until needed.

If using the beets, put them in a shallow bowl and pour the vinegar over them. Let sit in the vinegar while you arrange the plates; they only need a few minutes.

To serve, arrange a few slices of salmon on each of 4 plates and put a generous dollop of compound butter next to it. Scatter a few croutons on each plate and garnish with the

SERVES 4

½ cup sea salt

⅓ cup packed dark brown sugar

4 tablespoons chopped fresh dill

1 shot glass (3 tablespoons) vodka (optional) (see Notes, page 24)

Grated zest of 3 lemons (about 3 tablespoons)

2 tablespoons prepared grated horseradish (see Notes, page 24)

One 12-ounce boneless, skinless salmon fillet

2 to 3 slices pumpernickel bread, trimmed and cut into cubes (about 2 cups)

1 tablespoon extra-virgin olive oil

1 tablespoon minced garlic

1 teaspoon minced yellow onion

1 tablespoon finely chopped fresh flat-leaf parsley

½ cup (1 stick) butter, at room temperature

1 cup cooked beet rounds (optional) (see Notes, page 24)

¼ cup champagne vinegar

½ cup mustard oil

1 tablespoon wild celery flowers, for garnish (optional)

remaining 2 tablespoons of dill and 1 tablespoon (or so) of zest and a drizzle of mustard oil. Garnish further with the beets and the celery flowers, if desired.

———

Notes: If you decide to leave out the vodka, neither the flavor nor the texture of the salmon will be affected. Sure, it adds a little flavor, but not so much that you need to worry about it. You may think you need to replace the 3 tablespoons of liquid, but you don't. Rest assured, the salmon will be a treat with or without vodka.

While most of us think of prepared horseradish as being somewhat creamy and cured in vinegar (white horseradish) or beet juice (red horseradish), you can also buy grated horseradish in jars, although it's not as common. If you can't find grated horseradish, buy a fresh root of horseradish, peel it, and use a vegetable grater to prepare it. If you've never done this before,

be warned: The fresh root is pungent—worse than chopping a strong onion!

You'll need about 8 ounces beets for 1 cup of sliced, cooked beets. If your beets weigh a little more, great. You'll just have more beets to eat. They are good boiled in water, like potatoes, or you can roast them. To boil, put the beets (whole and unpeeled) in a large saucepan filled with boiling salted water. Let the water return to a boil and cook for about 30 minutes for medium-size beets, or until the beets are tender when pierced with a fork. To roast them, spread the beets in a roasting pan and roast for about 45 minutes at 350°F, or until they are fork-tender. Adjust the cooking time up or down about 10 minutes for large or small beets. Let the cooked beets cool, and then slip off their skins (much easier than trying to peel them before they're cooked). Slice into ¼- to ½-inch-thick rounds and you're in business.

You might call this bruschetta, or even "lazy pizza." Fine with me! Call it anything, but try it sooner rather than later. Finishing it with Calabrian chili oil "Blais-es" it up with a little unexpected fire. Friends, read more about this amazing oil on page 121, and try to keep a bottle in your fridge at all times. I like it with whole, long peppers in the oil.

TOMATOES AND BURRATA

Fill a large saucepan about halfway with water and bring to a boil over high heat. Set a bowl near the stove and fill it with ice and cold water.

Carefully drop the tomatoes in the boiling water and blanch for 2 minutes. Using a slotted spoon, lift the tomatoes from the boiling water and submerge them in the ice water. Let chill for 1 minute, lift from the water, and drain on thick kitchen towels.

Put the onion rings and tomatoes in a mixing bowl and add the olive oil and vinegar. Season to taste with salt and pepper and toss gently to coat the onions and tomatoes. Set aside for at least 5 minutes to marinate.

In a mixing bowl, whisk the burrata until the skin breaks down and the cheese is fluffy and creamy.

Spread the cheese on the toasts and then arrange them on a serving platter. Lift the onions and tomatoes from the dressing and distribute them over the toasts. Drizzle with the chili oil and garnish with the basil. Serve immediately.

SERVES 4

4 cups cherry tomatoes

2 red onions, sliced into ¼-inch-thick rings

¼ cup extra-virgin olive oil

2 tablespoons red wine vinegar

Kosher salt and freshly ground black pepper

8 to 10 ounces burrata (You only need 8 ounces, but who can resist snacking? Better to have a few spare ounces!)

4 slices ciabatta bread, each about ¼ inch thick, toasted

2 teaspoons Calabrian chili oil (see Note, page 121)

½ cup whole fresh basil leaves

Anchovies make a statement, no way around it, and the statement is "I know what's up!" Chefs love the tiny little fish, especially when they're brined or otherwise salted. Here they provide a piquant contrast to a velvety hummus made from fava beans (another chef favorite). I call for 24 swimmers here, but the number depends on how fond you are of the little guys. My rule? Use enough to ensure a taste of anchovy in each bite but not so many that you barely taste the hummus. The radish coins provide crunchy bitterness and the orange, acidic sweetness. A lot going on with these toasts.

Another thing that I love about the spread is that you just might have the ingredients lying around the kitchen. And if not? Sub chickpeas for favas, a regular ole orange for the blood orange, and a shot of fish sauce for the anchovies. That kind of thinking epitomizes so much of what cooking is about: constantly adapting and evolving. On the other hand, if you find yourself with fresh favas in the springtime, use them. Why not? (See the Notes at the end of the recipe for how.)

If you find yourself with a few extra minutes, sprinkle some cracked coriander seeds and sliced radish leaves over the toasts, and drizzle sherry vinegar on them. These garnishes take them to the next level.

FAVA BEAN HUMMUS
WITH WHITE ANCHOVIES

SERVES 4

2 cups cooked fava beans (see Notes)

2 cloves garlic, minced

Juice of 2 lemons (about 4 tablespoons)

2 tablespoons mayonnaise

¼ cup extra-virgin olive oil

Kosher salt

4 large baguette slices, about ¼ inch thick, toasted

24 white anchovy fillets (see Notes)

10 to 12 radishes, cut into ¼-inch-thick coins (about 1 cup)

2 blood oranges, peeled and segmented

½ cup chopped fresh flat-leaf parsley (about ⅓ bunch)

In a blender, mix the favas, garlic, lemon juice, and mayonnaise and blend until smooth. With the motor running, drizzle the olive oil through the lid into the blender until the hummus is blended. Season to taste with salt and pulse to mix. (Don't let the blender spin for longer than necessary, as it can actually "cook" or discolor the hummus, or even make it taste bitter.)

Spread the hummus evenly on the toast slices. Drape the anchovies over the hummus in a slightly overlapping pattern, like a shingled roof. Garnish with the radish coins, blood orange segments, and parsley. Serve immediately.

Notes: I developed this recipe with cooked frozen favas, which work well, as do canned favas. I did this to save you the trouble of prepping fresh favas, but without question, they are excellent in this recipe. You'll have to liberate them from their pods and then blanch them in simmering salted water for about 3 minutes. Drain and plunge the beans into ice water to stop the cooking. When they're cool, peel away the shell on each bean. Then you're ready to go.

I suggest you use mild white anchovies for this small plate, which in the U.S. are often called boquerones and refer to the Spanish anchovies packed in vinegar and salt in small glass jars or small plastic tubs.

GUACAMOLE

Who doesn't like guac? Here's my take on the ridiculously rich indulgence.

SERVES 3 TO 5

3 avocados, pitted and peeled

Juice of 2 limes

1 red onion, chopped

1 bunch fresh cilantro, chopped

1 clove garlic, finely chopped

Pinch of cayenne pepper (optional)

Kosher salt

Put the avocados in a mixing bowl and immediately sprinkle with the lime juice to prevent browning.

Using a potato masher or fork, mash the avocados until nearly smooth. Fold in the onion, cilantro, and garlic. Season to taste with cayenne, if using, and salt.

PICO DE GALLO

My version of the popular tomato-based salsa, with a kick from jalapeños. If you add peas, it becomes pea-co de gallo.

SERVES 4 TO 6

8 Roma tomatoes, chopped

2 white onions, chopped

1 bunch fresh cilantro, chopped

2 jalapeños, seeded and stems removed, finely chopped (see Note)

2 limes

Kosher salt

In a mixing bowl, stir together the tomatoes, onions, cilantro, and jalapeños. Squeeze the juice from the limes over the pico de gallo. Stir, season to taste with salt, and serve.

___

Note: For a spicier pico de gallo, leave some or all the seeds in the jalapeños.

Despite the relatively long list of ingredients, this is about as easy a tuna first course as you can find. Plus, it showcases really good tuna—served nearly raw yet seared just enough to give the fish a pretty and tasty finish. The Asian hints are just right with the tuna and tomatoes. (For more on choosing the tuna, see the Notes at the end of the recipe.)

TUNA STEAK TATAKI
AND HEIRLOOM TOMATO CRUDO

In a small bowl, mix together the garlic, sesame seeds, onion powder, togarashi, if using, and about 1 teaspoon salt. Sprinkle this seasoning mix on both sides of the tuna, gently pressing the mix into the tuna.

Heat a large nonstick skillet over high heat. Sear the tuna blocks just until they brown slightly, 1½ to 2 minutes on each side. Remove from the pan and slice the seared tuna into slices. These can be thick-ish, ¼ to ½ inch thick.

Slice the tomatoes into pieces of similar size and put in a mixing bowl. Season aggressively with salt and then sprinkle with the yuzu, oil, and soy sauce. Season with pepper and toss gently. Add the shiso and toss again.

Arrange the tuna slices on plates and spoon the tomatoes next to them. Serve immediately.

Notes: Any sushi-grade tuna can be used here; ask the fishmonger to cut it into bricks that weigh about 12 ounces each. You can also buy saku blocks, which are part of a sushi chef's pantry: flash-frozen sushi-grade yellowtail tuna. The blocks weigh between 10 and 14 ounces and are cut so that all are the same size, approximately 6 inches long by 3 inches wide by 1 inch thick.

White soy sauce is also called shoyu and is used widely in Japan, if not in the rest of the world. It has a mild flavor and is more transparent and thinner than other soy sauces. Look for it in Asian markets and online, although some supermarkets carry it.

SERVES 4

2 cloves garlic, minced

4 teaspoons sesame seeds

2 teaspoons onion powder

1 teaspoon togarashi (optional) (see Note, page 141)

Kosher salt

4 saku yellowtail tuna blocks, thawed, if necessary (see Notes)

1 pint cherry or grape tomatoes (choose the ripest and most appealing tomatoes)

2 tablespoons yuzu juice

2 teaspoons dark sesame oil

1 to 2 teaspoons white soy sauce (also called shoyu) (see Notes)

Freshly ground black pepper

1 to 2 tablespoons torn or coarsely chopped fresh green shiso, basil, or cilantro, for garnish (see Note, page 89)

This one is so femme, it could be served in the dressing room at Anthropologie. Being so easy, light, and airy, it's a perfect Sunday brunch dish. The key is to cook the grapes long and hot enough so that they shrivel and resemble olives. This culinary illusion elevates the sweetness of the toasts because you expect salty, not sweet, when you bite into one.

CONCORD GRAPES
AND RICOTTA TOASTS

SERVES 5 OR 6

5 or 6 thick slices sourdough bread

5 cups ricotta cheese, drained in a colander for about 1 hour

Grated zest and juice of 3 large lemons

Kosher salt

8 cups Concord grapes (3½ to 4 pounds)

¼ cup Concord grape vinegar or balsamic vinegar

Mustard flowers, for garnish (optional)

Preheat the oven to 400°F.

Grill or toast the bread until golden. Set aside.

In a mixing bowl, stir the ricotta with the lemon zest and juice and a pinch of salt.

Spread the grapes in a single layer on a baking sheet, sprinkle with a little salt, and roast for about 1 minute. Turn off the oven and let the grapes sit in the hot oven until wrinkled and softened, about 10 minutes.

Spread the ricotta on the toast and then top with the roasted grapes. Drizzle with the vinegar, garnish with mustard flowers, if using, and serve.

Let's face it, we're a nation built on corn, and these little guys represent all that is perfect about one of our truest American ingredients. Sweet, milky, and earthy . . . and fried! I triple-dog-dare you to eat just one, especially when you pair the warm fitters with the lime crema. Mexican crema is in the cooler of your local tienda, and probably in your supermarket, too. If you must, substitute crème fraîche for the crema. It will do very well!

CORN FRITTERS
WITH MEXICAN CREMA

In a deep, heavy pot or deep-fat fryer, heat the oil over medium-high heat until it registers 350°F on a deep-frying thermometer.

In a mixing bowl, whisk together the flour, baking powder, ½ teaspoon salt, and the sugar.

In another bowl, whisk together the eggs, milk, and butter. Pour the dry ingredients into the milk mixture and stir until blended. Gently fold in the corn.

In a mixing bowl, whisk together the crema and lime zest and juice.

Working in batches, drop spoonfuls of the batter into the hot oil and fry until golden brown, 3 to 5 minutes, using tongs or long chopsticks to turn the fritters and ensure even browning. Lift the fritters from the oil with a slotted spoon and drain on paper towels. Lightly season the fritters with salt. Let the oil regain its temperature between batches. Serve the warm fritters with the lime crema.

Note: Mexican crema is similar to crème fraîche and sour cream, although it's a little thinner than either—plus it's somewhat acidic and a little saltier. If you can't find it in the market, substitute sour cream cut with a little lime juice and seasoned with salt.

SERVES 4

About 2 quarts vegetable oil

1 cup all-purpose flour

1 teaspoon baking powder

Kosher salt

¼ teaspoon sugar

4 large eggs

½ cup whole or 2% milk

1 tablespoon unsalted butter, melted

About 2 cups corn kernels (one 16-ounce bag frozen corn)

1 cup Mexican crema or crème fraîche

Grated zest and juice of 2 limes

Have you stood in line for more than an hour at the halal food stand on 53rd Street in Manhattan? Me neither! And there's no reason to when you can put together its specialty in just 15 minutes. An outdoor grill will give the chicken an authentic char and flavor, but a stovetop grill pan does a very good job, too. If there's time and room, toss the pitas on the heat for about a minute to maximize their flavor. And, don't forget to give the grill a chance to get hot before you start.

Before we go any further, I gotta come clean: I *have* endured a ridiculously long wait for chicken shawarma at that halal stand. It was delicious! The good news is, my recipe duplicates it so you can avoid the wait. You're welcome.

CHICKEN SHAWARMA

In a large mixing bowl, whisk together the olive oil, cumin, paprika, allspice, turmeric, garlic powder, and cinnamon. Season with salt and pepper. Add the chicken and turn to coat thoroughly. Set aside.

In another mixing bowl, stir together the yogurt, lime juice, and garlic. Season to taste with salt and pepper.

Prepare a gas or charcoal grill so that the heating element or coals are medium-hot. Alternatively, heat a grill pan over medium-high heat until hot.

Lift the chicken from the marinade and grill for 5 to 7 minutes on each side, until nicely charred and cooked through. Transfer to a platter and cover with aluminum foil. Let the chicken rest for about 5 minutes.

Slice the chicken into strips and pile them evenly on the pitas. Top the chicken with the mint and cilantro and drizzle each serving with the yogurt sauce.

SERVES 4

¼ cup extra-virgin olive oil

2 teaspoons ground cumin

2 teaspoons sweet paprika

1 teaspoon ground allspice

½ teaspoon ground turmeric

¼ teaspoon garlic powder

¼ teaspoon ground cinnamon

Kosher salt and freshly ground black pepper

6 boneless, skinless chicken thighs

1 cup plain whole-milk Greek yogurt

Juice of 2 limes

1 clove garlic, minced

6 pita breads

¼ cup chopped fresh mint leaves

¼ cup chopped fresh cilantro leaves

I once made these rellenos for about 500 people in Aspen, Colorado. At that volume, the effort was high-level laborious—as you can imagine. Yet making the fried blossoms for a few friends is a breeze, or at least a lot easier than you might think. What I love about the dish is that on their own the stuffed blossoms are incredibly precious and very Northern California . . . very Alice Waters . . . very Zuni Café. But I turn the delicate flowers into rellenos by coating and then frying them, which gives them the street grit they need. A real NorCal-SoCal collabo.

SQUASH BLOSSOM
RELLENOS

SERVES 4

4 poblano peppers, each about 5 inches long

1 quart peanut oil

¼ cup grated Monterey Jack cheese

32 zucchini blossoms, stamens removed

12 large egg whites (2 cups)

1 cup masa harina

Kosher salt

Heat a large cast-iron skillet over high heat.

Coat the peppers with some of the oil and roast them in the hot skillet, turning until charred on all sides. Alternatively, roast the peppers over an open flame, holding them with long-handled tongs and turning until charred. Transfer the peppers to a glass bowl and cover with plastic wrap. Set aside for 5 to 10 minutes to give the peppers time to steam.

Using your fingers, peel the charred skin from the peppers. Cut them into small dice. Put the diced peppers in a mixing bowl, add the cheese, and mix well.

Using a small spoon, carefully stuff the cheese mixture into the squash blossoms. If they tear a little, don't worry, but try to keep rips to a minimum.

In a deep, heavy pot, heat the oil over medium-high heat until the oil registers 350°F on a deep-frying thermometer.

Meanwhile, whisk the egg whites in a shallow bowl until frothy. Put the masa harina in another shallow bowl.

Dip the stuffed blossoms first into the egg whites and then into the masa to coat both sides.

In batches so as not to crowd the pan, gently slip the coated blossoms into the hot oil and fry until golden brown, 2 to 3 minutes, using long-handled tongs or chopsticks to turn them so that they brown evenly. Drain the blossoms on paper towels.

Immediately season the blossoms with salt and serve hot.

A small-town Long Island boy's first vivid food memory is of eating stuffed clams with his family at a random clam bar on the South Shore. Twenty years later, I took that memory to the West Coast and created new memories for the next generation. Abalone might be harder to source and deal with than clams (which make an acceptable sub), but if you do find it, here's a lowbrow approach to a notoriously high-end seafood. Can't manage the lemon foam? Settle for a squeeze of lemon—although using a siphon is easy and oh-so-satisfying.

ABALONE STUFFIES

For the lemon foam, in a saucepan, combine 6 tablespoons water, the sugar, and the gelatin sheets and warm over medium-low heat until the sugar and gelatin dissolve. Let the syrup cool, and then refrigerate for at least 1 hour or until cold.

Stir the egg whites and lemon juice into the syrup. Whisk until fully incorporated. Pour the mixture into a chilled whipping siphon or iSi siphon.

For the stuffies, turn on the broiler and set the rack a few inches from it, leaving enough room for the broiler pan.

Heat the oil in a medium sauté pan over medium-high heat. Add the pancetta, onions, celery, and garlic and cook, stirring, until fragrant and the vegetables begin to soften, 3 to 4 minutes. Season to taste with salt and pepper.

Stir in the abalone and stock and cook, stirring occasionally, for 2 minutes longer. Add the panko, cheese, and 2 tablespoons of the parsley. Season to taste with salt and pepper.

Pack the stuffing into each of the clamshells, making a nice little mound. Top each with a pat of butter and a grating of Parmesan. Arrange the packed shells on a broiler pan and slide it under the broiler. Broil for about 5 minutes, until the filling is golden brown and the butter bubbles.

Charge the filled siphon with one nitrous oxide gas charge. Shake well and discharge the foam onto the hot abalone mixture. Garnish with the remaining 1 tablespoon parsley and serve.

———

Note: Abalone, a shellfish greatly prized on the West Coast of the United States, can be found in other parts of the world as well, although it's becoming increasingly rare and therefore hard to find. A single-shell mollusk, it can grow to be quite large, although the abalone you'll want here should be about the size of a bar of soap. With luck, you'll get abalone shells along with it. If you can't find it fresh (which may not be easy), it's available frozen and even canned. Substitute 32 cherrystone or top-neck clams (really any clams that you can find in the shell). You will need to add about a cup of chopped clams to round out the meat, since abalone are meatier than clams.

SERVES 4 TO 6

LEMON FOAM

2 tablespoons sugar

2 sheets gelatin

4 large egg whites (½ cup)

½ cup fresh lemon juice (from 3 or 4 lemons)

STUFFIES

1 tablespoon olive oil

2 ounces pancetta, sliced

½ cup minced yellow onions (about ½ medium onion)

¼ cup minced celery (about 1 stalk)

2 cloves garlic, minced

Kosher salt and freshly ground black pepper

32 abalone, shelled, cleaned, and chopped (see Note)

¼ cup vegetable stock, preferably homemade

1 cup panko bread crumbs

½ cup grated Parmesan cheese, plus more for topping

3 tablespoons chopped fresh flat-leaf parsley

32 clamshells, cleaned

6 tablespoons (¾ stick) unsalted butter, at room temperature

If you've seen the movie *The Life Aquatic with Steve Zissou*, you'll get what I mean when I say this recipe is Zissou-inspired. In the movie, sea animals are called "creatures"—I love that. Squid is a little creepy, right? So it works as a "creature." Feel free to substitute your preferred "creatures" (clams, scallops, even crawfish!), or rely on those I call for here. This is meant to be served right out of the frying fat, resting on newspapers and sprinkled with lemon juice and seaweed salt. Okay! Seaweed salt is a little over the top; kosher salt is good.

FRIED SEA CREATURES
WITH AVOCADO TARTAR SAUCE

SERVES 4

In a small mixing bowl, whisk together the yogurt, lime zest and juice, cilantro, capers, parsley, and garlic. Gently fold in the avocado and set aside.

Spread the cornmeal on a large plate and season generously with salt and pepper. Stir to mix.

Pour the buttermilk into a large bowl. Whisk in a few teaspoons of the chili oil until fully incorporated and the buttermilk is as spicy as you like.

Working with one piece at a time, dip the calamari, shrimp, and oysters into the buttermilk and then coat on both sides with the cornmeal. Arrange the coated seafood on a wax paper–lined tray, in preparation for frying.

Pour the oil into a large, heavy pot to a depth of about 3 inches. Heat over medium-high heat until a deep-frying thermometer registers 350°F.

Shake each piece of seafood to remove excess cornmeal and gently drop into the hot oil. Fry until golden brown. Do not fry all the pieces at once; you do not want to crowd the pot. Using a slotted spoon, lift the fried seafood from the pot and drain on newspapers or paper towels.

Season with salt to taste, a squeeze of lemon, and the chopped dill or parsley. Serve hot, with the tartar sauce.

3 tablespoons plain whole-milk Greek yogurt

Grated zest and juice of 1 lime

2 tablespoons chopped fresh cilantro

2 tablespoons drained capers

1 tablespoon chopped fresh flat-leaf parsley

1 clove garlic, minced

1 avocado, pitted, peeled, and diced

2 cups cornmeal

Kosher salt and freshly ground black pepper

2 cups buttermilk

Calabrian chili oil, as needed (see Note, page 121)

8 calamari bodies, cut into rings

8 large shrimp, peeled and deveined

4 oysters, shucked

Vegetable oil, for frying

½ lemon

2 tablespoons chopped fresh dill or flat-leaf parsley

SHRIMP—Not So Skimpy

For many years, shrimp was considered fancy and reserved for special occasions. The plump little bites of pink luxury were often served on chipped ice with red cocktail sauce or in a garlic-laced dish called scampi. (This gave birth to a series of shrimp "skimpy" jokes, but never mind.) Those days are long gone—today shrimp are everywhere and always. They reign as our favorite seafood; I've read that we average about four pounds of shrimp a year per person, which adds up to something like a billion pounds. Nothing skimpy about those numbers.

I'm right there with everyone else. I love shrimp for its versatility, mild brininess, and irresistible texture. I like how it's such a cooperative partner for, say, a righteous green garlic butter (page 49) or how it pairs with the boldness of beer and Worcestershire sauce (page 111).

Like all love affairs, ours with shrimp has its costs. It's all about how the shrimp are raised or caught. Fact is, most of the shrimp we eat comes from Asia, where gigantic farms produce hundreds of thousands of shrimp to feed our habit. Big business for many, yet regulation is often lacking overseas, and consequently the shrimp are treated with antibiotics and other chemicals to kill bacteria that you might not be keen to ingest.

What to do? Buy American.

American (and European) shrimp farms are held to pretty strict standards and produce healthy crustaceans. A few are closed-systems operations, which are the most environmentally sound. And when it's not farmed, shrimp is caught in the warm waters of the Gulf of Mexico or off the coasts of South Carolina and Georgia. They're harvested in trawl nets, which these days are thankfully fitted with devices that reduce the amount of bycatch scooped up in the nets. This is where the Monterey Bay Aquarium's Seafood Watch app comes to the rescue. It will tell you which shrimp—and other fish and seafood—are currently plentiful and safe to eat.

It's always a good idea to buy shrimp in the shell and shell them yourselves. Yes, it's a little more time-consuming, but the shrimp will taste better and have a more appealing texture. Most shrimp have been flash frozen and then defrosted and it's not a good idea to refreeze them, and so if you want to stock up on shrimp, buy them already frozen. And when you buy defrosted or fresh shrimp, cook them within a day.

Shrimp come in different sizes, with the most popular being jumbo and large, although you can sometimes find medium shrimp and even smaller. They are sized by how many are in a pound: 10 to 15 per pound for jumbo; 16 to 20 for large; and 25 to 30 for medium. Small shrimp are often called bay shrimp. We may refer to jumbo shrimp as prawns—not precisely accurate, but a nice turn of phrase and a good way to indicate you're looking for the big guys.

In the end, it's not easy to know if the shrimp you buy come from the United States, which is why it's a good idea to talk to the guy behind the counter at the market. Let him know you're interested in American shrimp. You might have to spend a little more, but that will just mean you're hipster retro: Shrimp is reserved for special occasions again.

Yes. You're reading the recipe right. I call for live prawns (or live jumbo shrimp), which goes against everything I believe about pretentious chef traits. Where the heck are you supposed to find live shrimp anyhow? Who has time to track them down? And yet, I say: Please try! I'd love you to experience this at least once in your life, so befriend a shrimper, get on a boat, hit up a chef you might know. Whatever it takes.

On the other hand, if you can only find the non-living variety of frozen or fresh shrimp, they will be tasty cooked like this with the green garlic butter. Just be sure to buy them in the shell. I like to make this with springtime's mild green garlic, but if you must, rely on regular ole garlic. Just use half as much. And a few charred lemon halves add interest to the presentation.

PRAWNS WITH
GREEN GARLIC BUTTER

Put the butter, garlic, lemon zest and juice, salt, and pepper in the bowl of a food processor fitted with the metal blade. Pulse until smooth.

Heat a grill pan over high heat until very hot. Using a long-handled brush, carefully coat the pan with the olive oil.

Put the live prawns on a cutting board and, with a very sharp knife, slice them in half lengthwise.

Immediately put the prawns on the hot pan and spoon some of the green butter on top of them. Cook until pink, 2 to 3 minutes on each side. When cooked through, serve the shrimp, flesh side up, with any remaining butter on top. Serve with parsley, if desired.

SERVES 4

1 cup (2 sticks) high-quality unsalted butter

¼ cup sliced green garlic, or 2 tablespoons sliced garlic

Grated zest and juice of 4½ lemons

1 teaspoon kosher salt

½ teaspoon freshly ground black pepper

2 tablespoons extra-virgin olive oil

16 live prawns or jumbo shrimp

Chopped fresh flat-leaf parsley, for garnish (optional)

I've toyed with dozens of versions of beef tartare, a carnal, crave-worthy dish for me. Sometimes I imagine I'm a lion (my spirit animal, naturally) enjoying a fresh kill. This version of tartare, featuring jalapeños and radishes, is a tip of the sombrero to Mexico. The gently fried eggs on top of the tartare make this dish especially luscious—even worthy of a hip restaurant. In fact, I've sold thousands of these at Juniper and Ivy, one of my San Diego restaurants.

CARNE ASADA
STEAK TARTARE AND EGGS

SERVES 4

8 ounces eye of round or another inexpensive cut of beef

¼ cup grated cloves garlic (9 or 10 cloves)

3 tablespoons crumbed cotija or feta cheese

4 or 5 radishes, finely diced

3 tablespoons thinly sliced scallions

1 fresh jalapeño, seeded and finely diced

1 red bell pepper, seeded and thinly sliced

Grated zest and juice of 1 lime

2 tablespoons olive oil

Kosher salt and freshly ground black pepper

Four ¼-inch-thick slices sourdough bread, toasted

4 tablespoons Mexican crema (see Note, page 34)

4 large eggs

Fresh cilantro flowers or fresh cilantro leaves, for garnish (optional)

Using a sharp knife, cut the beef into small dice. Next, aggressively pass the knife through the meat to mince it so that it has the texture of raw ground meat. Transfer to a large bowl.

Add the garlic, cheese, radishes, scallions, jalapeño, bell pepper, lime zest and juice, and 1 tablespoon of the olive oil. Season with salt and pepper and mix together with a spoon, or your hands if you are really invested. Refrigerate for at least 1 hour to chill. If short on time, freeze for 5 to 10 minutes.

Arrange the toasts on a platter and spread 1 tablespoon of the Mexican crema evenly over each slice. Remove the meat from the fridge, taste and adjust the seasonings if necessary, and spread it evenly on the toasts, gently packing so that the toppings will not fall off.

Heat a large nonstick sauté pan over low heat. Add the remaining 1 tablespoon olive oil and, when hot, fry the eggs until the whites are completely set. Cover the sauté pan to steam the yolks. They should be fluid but not runny when they are done. (I like to say they are "pliable.") Season the eggs with salt and pepper and position an egg on top of each toast.

If you still have time on the clock, for some extra flavor, grab some cilantro flowers from your garden or chop some fresh cilantro leaves to garnish the eggs and tartare.

Lobster, meet mayo. Who could have predicted that this personal introduction that I made years ago would have evolved into such an amazing marriage of flavor? I'm such a mensch . . . and a liar, obviously! This outstanding combo goes way, way back, before my time. The beauty—and success—of the dish is that it doesn't require too many ingredients. You want the tang of the pickled celery (celery is an excellent ingredient for quick pickling because it already has a nice natural salinity) and a good slather of mayo (primarily because everything is better with a good slather of mayo) and lots of dill.

A bit of fresh tarragon and dill, and a drizzle of good mustard oil—the kind that happily burns into your nasal passages—make great finishes, but in the end this recipe is beautiful in its simplicity: the jeans and T-shirt of food.

LOBSTER AND CELERY

In a large saucepan, place the celery root and enough cold water to cover by 2 to 3 inches. Add 1 tablespoon salt and bring to a boil over medium-high heat. Cook the celery root until fork-tender, about 25 minutes. Drain and then coarsely cut the celery root into several pieces. Transfer the pieces to the bowl of a food processor fitted with the metal blade. Pulse several times or until the celery root is smooth. Set aside.

Put the celery stalks in a large bowl and sprinkle with 1 tablespoon salt. Let sit for 5 minutes, and then rinse the celery under running water.

In a large saucepan, combine the sugar and vinegar with 1 cup water. Bring to a simmer over medium heat and cook, stirring occasionally, until the sugar dissolves and the mixture boils. Pour the hot liquid over the celery stalks and set aside. (You can buy Andy Ricker's Pok Pok Som Chinese celery vinegar instead and

splash it over the raw celery and forget all this boiling and stirring and mixing: a major shortcut that intensifies the flavor quickly.)

Heat a large sauté pan over medium-high heat. Add the buns cut side down and toast until golden. Liberally butter the toasted sides of the buns and return them to the pan, buttered sides up, to toast the outsides for just a minute or so, until golden brown and the butter melts.

Put the lobster in a mixing bowl. Add the mayonnaise and lemon juice and mix gently with a wooden spoon. Stir in the pureed celery root, taking care not to break up the lobster meat more than can be helped. Toss in the celery leaves and tarragon. Season with salt and pepper to taste.

Divide the lobster salad among the buns and garnish with the dill fronds and a drizzle of mustard oil or mustard caviar. Serve immediately, with the pickled celery on the side.

SERVES 4

1 small celery root, peeled and cut into 2 or 3 chunks

Kosher salt

8 stalks celery, cut into 2- to 3-inch lengths

1 cup sugar

2 cups apple cider vinegar

4 brioche buns, split

3 to 4 tablespoons unsalted butter, softened

1½ pounds cooked lobster knuckle meat, coarsely chopped

⅓ cup mayonnaise

2 teaspoons fresh lemon juice

⅓ cup chopped celery leaves

3 sprigs fresh tarragon, leaves chopped

Freshly ground black pepper

¼ cup fresh dill fronds

Mustard oil or mustard caviar (pickled mustard seeds), for garnish

Dill flowers, for garnish (optional)

Living in Southern California has its benefits. Of the highest order is the amazing seafood and access to the Baja peninsula. Ensenada, a quaint little coastal spot on Mexico's Baja Peninsula, boasts Mediterranean-like weather and a thriving food and wine culture. This raw albacore dish is a riff on a traditional Ensenada classic.

It relies on a blending of the Japanese chili paste called *yuzu kosho* (see the Notes) and Kewpie mayo for a spread with a satisfying hit of green Mexi-terranean heat. Sub in your favorite regional mayo if you can't find Kewpie. Top the tuna with quick-pickled onion and lots of cilantro leaves and stems. Yes! I said *stems*. There's way too much flavor in those stems to waste them, plus they add a distinct textural element. A sliced avocado would be a nice addition, too, and in keeping with the origin of this. Outrageous eating experience.

ALBACORE TUNA
TOSTADAS

In a small bowl, whisk together the scallions, cilantro, coriander, cumin, and the ¼ cup olive oil. Set aside.

Drizzle a little olive oil over the tuna and season lightly with salt and pepper.

In another small bowl, stir together the mayonnaise and *yuzu kosho*. Add the lime juice and mix the aioli well. Spread the aioli evenly over each warm tortilla.

Divide the tuna among the warm tortillas and season with salt and a drizzle of the scallion-cilantro oil. Garnish with the pickled onions and cilantro leaves (or cilantro flowers) and serve before the tortillas cool.

Notes: Supersmooth Kewpie mayonnaise is a popular brand in Japan that's made with rice vinegar.

Yuzu kosho is a spicy Japanese green chili paste flavored with citrusy yuzu. It's available in Asian markets and online. You can substitute sambal or another Asian chili sauce, but take a good look for *yuzu kosho*.

If you're pressed for time (and who isn't?), you can make a delicious pickling brine by mixing ½ cup vinegar with ¼ cup salt and a good squeeze of honey. Pour this over the onions and let them sit for a while. One more word about pickling: It's easy to double or triple the recipe to make extra. And why not? Pickled red onions add good flavor to sandwiches, salads, grills, and on and on.

SERVES 4

¼ cup minced scallions

3 tablespoons ½-inch-long fresh cilantro stems and leaves, plus more for garnish (or use fresh cilantro flowers if you can find them)

1 tablespoon coriander seeds, toasted and crushed

1 tablespoon cumin seeds, toasted and crushed

¼ cup extra-virgin olive oil, plus more for drizzling

12 ounces albacore tuna, shaved sashimi-style or sliced into ¼-inch-thick rectangles, or as close as you can manage

Kosher salt and freshly ground black pepper

½ cup Kewpie mayonnaise (see Notes)

2 tablespoons yuzu kosho (see Notes)

Juice of 2 limes

Four 6-inch corn tortillas, warmed

½ cup Pickled Red Onions (page 217)

As a French Laundry alum, I've been remixing this Thomas Keller classic for years. This is my new . . . okay, it's my current version. By the time this book is published, I probably will have another "favorite." Because I grew up a typical American kid who had a fondness for jarred cocktail sauce, I decided to blend kimchi—which is made with fermented vegetables—with the flavors found in traditional cocktail sauce to create, yes, kimchi cocktail sauce!

Certainly, you don't have to freeze the sauce into "pearls," because the oysters will taste just as delicious if the cold sauce is dolloped on them. But if you really want to impress that friend in the science lab, smuggle some liquid nitrogen from any street corner in New York City, where liquid nitrogen is used to cool subway lines underground. Actually, don't do that—it sounds illegal. But you can buy liquid nitrogen and follow my instructions in the Note for quick-freezing the tasty little pearls.

OYSTERS WITH KIMCHI
COCKTAIL SAUCE

SERVES 4

¼ cup good-quality kimchi

2 tablespoons ketchup

2 tablespoons prepared chili sauce

2 tablespoons prepared horseradish

1 tablespoon red wine vinegar

Juice of 1 lemon

Kosher salt

16 oysters, shucked and bottom shells reserved (see Sidebar)

In a blender, combine the kimchi, ketchup, chili sauce, horseradish, vinegar, and lemon juice. Add a little salt to taste. Blend on high speed until smooth. The sauce should be the texture of household paint and slowly drip from the end of a spoon. If it's too thick, add a little water and blend until smooth; if it's too thin, add a little more kimchi and blend until smooth. Taste and adjust the seasonings. Cover and chill for at least 30 minutes and up to 4 hours.

Arrange the oyster shells on a serving plate and put an oyster in each one. (If you have chopped ice, set the oyster shells on a bed of it.) Spoon the kimchi sauce onto each. Serve immediately.

Note: To make frozen pearls, pour the sauce into a squeeze bottle. Put 2 quarts liquid nitrogen into a food-safe, rigid plastic or stainless steel container. Slowly drop the sauce from the squeeze bottle into the nitrogen to form "pearls." Garnish the oysters with them.

> » HOW TO SHUCK OYSTERS

When you want to shuck fresh, live oysters, first prepare a bed of crushed ice on a large rimmed platter. Scrub the oyster shells with a brush or scrubby towel under cool running water. Hold the oyster with the hinge facing you. Insert the tip of an oyster knife—or a butter knife if that's all you have, and it's all I've had many times—between the top and bottom shells at the joint. Gently twist the blade and pop the shells apart. Move the blade across the top of the shell to sever the muscle. Then gently position the knife under the oyster meat and sever the muscle from the bottom shell. Hold the oysters over a bowl while doing this so that you capture the liquor, which is where all the wonderful oceanic flavors reside; once the oysters are on ice, you can pour the liquid back over the muscle. Nestle the oysters in the bottom shells and set the shells on the crushed ice.

Young coconut is *not* the newest artist signed to Lil Wayne's record label, although I'm calling rights to that name just in case. Besides being an incredibly amazing hip-hop emcee name, young coconut is a special thing. Its flesh, both visually and texturally, looks like raw squid, which sounds either gross or mind-blowing. I realize there is no middle ground here. But the flavor of this dish is slamming and slurpingly tasty. Buy green coconuts filled with so much juice it swishes noisily around inside. Where to find young green coconuts? In Asian groceries and along the side of the road in Jamaica.

COCONUT NOODLES
WITH PEANUT SAUCE

Lay 1 coconut on its side. Using a large knife, chop off the pointed end by a few inches. Cut away the husk until you see the white, meaty flesh. Drain the coconut water into a container and reserve as a hydrating beverage for your marathon training, or as a hydrating beverage for finishing this recipe.

With a paring knife, gently remove the flesh from the shell. Try to keep it in long sheets, if possible. Lay the flesh on a large cutting board and slice it into 1/8-inch-wide "noodles." Put the noodles in a large mixing bowl. Repeat with the remaining 3 coconuts.

In a blender or the bowl of a food processor fitted with the metal blade, combine the peanut butter with the soy sauce, ginger, garlic, sriracha, sugar, fish sauce, and lime zest and juice. Pulse until smooth. The sauce should be the texture of heavy cream; add 1 tablespoon water if necessary to achieve this texture. Taste and adjust the seasonings.

Pour the peanut sauce over the coconut noodles and gently toss until they are thoroughly coated. Serve in bowls or in the coconut shells themselves, garnished with the cilantro and mint.

———

Note: Young coconuts are getting easier to find these days, and they're easier to cut than mature coconuts—which is good news, as you have to cut the coconut meat into "noodles." This could take a little while, but oh, man! Are these noodles tasty!

SERVES 4

4 young green coconuts (see Note)

1/2 cup peanut butter (creamy or chunky; your choice)

2 tablespoons soy sauce

1 tablespoon minced fresh ginger

1 teaspoon minced garlic

1 teaspoon sriracha sauce

1 teaspoon sugar

1 teaspoon fish sauce

Grated zest and juice of 1 lime

1 tablespoon chopped fresh cilantro flowers or leaves

1 tablespoon chopped fresh mint

Like much of my food, this is a mash-up of two different thought-trains colliding on a plate. In this case, the first is chilled, fatty slices of yellowtail that meet the second, classic Mediterranean flavors. This makes these one part ceviche, one part gyro—and all parts a super refreshing lunch. The red-hued Aleppo pepper adds a bit of zing and smokiness, and the pomegranate seeds provide a caviar-like pop of sweetness. Be generous with the herbs and lemon . . . but hey, be even more generous with the portions!

YELLOWTAIL WITH
SMOKED YOGURT AND POMEGRANATE SEEDS

In a small mixing bowl, whisk together the lemon juice, pomegranate juice, olive oil, Aleppo pepper, and a pinch of salt. Set aside.

Put the yogurt in a large shallow bowl. Cover with plastic wrap, leaving an opening to insert the nozzle of a handheld smoker (see Note). Fill the smoker with wood chips and light according to the manufacturer's instructions. Allow the bowl to fill with smoke, then remove the nozzle and seal the opening. Let the yogurt sit for 3 to 5 minutes before uncovering it.

Divide the yellowtail among 4 serving plates and drizzle with the Aleppo pepper vinaigrette.

Put a dollop of yogurt next to the fish and garnish with the pomegranate seeds, sorrel, parsley, and purslane, if using. Squeeze a little lemon juice over the fish and serve.

———

Note: Handheld smokers are available through Williams-Sonoma and similar companies. You will need the smoker, wood chips of your choice, and a lighter to get the full appeal of this. You could try to rig a smoker at home, although that sounds kind of dangerous. Liquid smoke? If you must . . . but it's not my first, second, or even thousandth choice.

SERVES 4

Juice of 2 lemons, plus more for serving

½ cup pomegranate juice

¼ cup extra-virgin olive oil

1 tablespoon Aleppo pepper

Sea salt

1 cup plain whole-milk Greek yogurt

Handful of applewood chips, for smoking

12 ounces yellowtail, sliced into ¼-inch-thick 2-inch-long planks

¼ cup pomegranate seeds

¼ cup torn sorrel leaves

¼ cup chopped fresh flat-leaf parsley or chervil

Sprigs of purslane, for garnish (optional)

SOUPS AND
A PORRIDGE

I am totally into soup these days, particularly hearty, rustic ones. In my first book, *Try This at Home*, there are recipes for lovely little pureed soups with fancy garnishes. All good, but by comparison, these soups are bigger, bolder, and ready for center stage.

These can be a full meal or a midnight snack. When I make a big pot of gumbo or *tom kha gai* (Thai chicken and coconut soup), my kids take it to school the next day in thermoses, echoing the meal from the night before: steaming bowls of soup and good bread. With all the broth, vegetables, fish, and meat in these soups, there are a couple of meals in each. Soup by Blais is global in breadth, local in execution, always personal, and downright delicious.

You'll probably find hominy in a big tin on a low shelf in the Latino section of the supermarket. Unfortunately, this section is often sadly small, yet hominy is nearly always available. Once you find it—and the Latino section in general—you will be super happy with all it has to offer. Some say pozole is great hangover food, but that puts it in a category far too narrow for its actual brilliance. My version is spicy and green, savory and salty, with an intense aroma. Don't forget to top the hearty soup with sliced radishes and shredded cabbage. A dollop of Mexican crema is always welcome, too.

SPICY GREEN POZOLE

Position the broiler rack a few inches from the heat source. Heat the broiler.

Spread the tomatillos, poblanos, and jalapeños on a baking sheet. Slide it under the broiler and let the vegetables char for 3 to 4 minutes, until blackened on one side. Turn the veggies and let them cook until blackened all the way around. Remove them from the broiler and let cool. When cool, seed the chiles and chop them and the tomatillos into small dice. Set aside.

Heat the oil in a large skillet over medium-high heat. When close to smoking, add the chicken thighs, skin sides down, and cook without moving the chicken until the skin starts to separate from the meat, 3 to 4 minutes. Turn the chicken over and add the onion and garlic to the skillet. Cook, stirring, until the onions are fragrant and translucent, 5 to 6 minutes.

Transfer the chicken, onions, and garlic to a large soup pot or similar pot. Add the charred chiles and tomatillos, the hominy, and then the stock. Bring to a boil, reduce the heat, and simmer until the chicken and hominy are cooked through and the flavors blend, 40 to 45 minutes, adjusting the heat up or down to maintain the simmer. Season to taste with salt and pepper.

Lift the chicken from the pot and, using a fork, shred the meat from the bones and return the meat to the soup. Discard the bones. Reheat the soup until very hot, if necessary.

Ladle the hot soup into large bowls and top each serving with a dollop of the crema, the cabbage, radishes, cilantro, scallions, and purslane, if using. Squeeze some lime into the bowls, garnish with jalapeños, and start slurping!

Note: Mildly sweet hominy is made from firm, dried corn kernels that have been soaked in an alkaline solution to slough off their hulls. It's used to make pozole, a traditional Mexican soup that always includes hominy and some sort of meat. The word *pozole* means "hominy."

SERVES 4 TO 6

5 or 6 tomatillos, husks removed

2 fresh poblano chiles

2 jalapeños

3 tablespoons olive oil

1 pound boneless, skinless chicken thighs

1 small yellow onion, diced

4 cloves garlic, minced

Two 15-ounce cans hominy (see Note)

1 quart chicken stock, preferably homemade

Kosher salt and freshly ground black pepper

About 1 cup Mexican crema (see Note, page 34)

2 cups shredded green cabbage (you can use red cabbage instead, but the soup is green, so the red veg will interfere with that)

1 cup radishes sliced 1/8 inch thick

Small handful of fresh cilantro stems and leaves

1 scallion, trimmed and thinly sliced, white and light green parts only

12 to 16 sprigs purslane (optional)

4 to 6 lime wedges

Sliced jalapeños, for garnish

Tortellini is the most storied pasta shape I know, and the broth here, inspired by the Vietnamese noodle soup called pho, is its perfect partner. It's at once soul satisfying and on trend with its aromatic spice infusion.

TORTELLINI WITH
BONE MARROW BROTH

To make the broth, preheat the oven to 375°F.

Spread the marrow bones on a baking sheet and roast until the bones brown and the marrow softens, 8 to 10 minutes. Remove the marrow bones from the oven and scoop out 2 tablespoons marrow if using it for the pasta dough.

Transfer the roasted marrow bones to a stockpot and add the onion, ginger, garlic, and star anise. Pour 1 gallon water over these ingredients and then add the parsley stems and salt. Bring to a rapid simmer over medium-high heat, but do not boil. Reduce the heat and simmer for about 1 hour.

Strain the stock through a colander and return the broth to the pot. Discard the solids. Add the fish sauce to the broth and bring to a rapid simmer over medium-high heat. Let the broth simmer briskly until reduced by one-third, about 10 minutes. Season to taste with salt, if necessary.

To make the pasta, pour the flour onto a clean work surface and make a well in the center. In a small bowl, mix the eggs, 2 tablespoons water, the marrow fat, if using, and salt. Pour the mixture into the flour well. Using two fingers, slowly incorporate the flour into the wet mixture until all of the liquid is absorbed and a supple dough is formed. Gather the dough into a ball and flatten into a disk. Wrap the dough in plastic wrap and refrigerate for 1 hour to rest.

Alternatively, put the flour in the bowl of a food processor fitted with the metal blade. With the motor running, pour the wet ingredients through the food tube. The dough is ready when it starts to pull away from the sides of the bowl.

To make the filling, in a mixing bowl, stir together the ricotta, Parmesan, parsley leaves, one of the eggs, the lemon juice, nutmeg, salt, and pepper.

Take the pasta dough from the refrigerator and roll it into sheets using a pasta machine. Alternatively, knead the dough on a lightly floured surface for 6 to 8 minutes and then roll into sheets with a rolling pin until they are about ⅛ inch thick (a little thicker won't matter).

In a small bowl, stir together the remaining egg and 1 teaspoon water.

Cut the pasta into 4-inch rounds with a cookie cutter or the rim of a glass. You will have about 25 rounds. Lay them on a floured work surface and scoop a small amount of filling in the center of each round. Brush the edges of the dough with the egg wash and fold in half to seal. Put a finger in the center of the seal and fold the dough back around your finger. Fold

BROTH

2 pounds meaty bone marrow or beef bones, cut into pieces (see Notes)

1 yellow or white onion, halved and charred (see Notes)

2- to 3-inch knob fresh ginger, sliced into 5 or 6 quarter-size pieces

2 cloves garlic

2 star anise

1 bunch fresh flat-leaf parsley stems (use the leaves for the tortellini filling)

Pinch of kosher salt

2½ tablespoons fish sauce

PASTA

2 cups all-purpose flour

2 large eggs

2 tablespoons bone marrow, melted, or olive oil (optional)

½ teaspoon kosher salt

FILLING

1 cup ricotta cheese

¼ cup freshly grated Parmesan cheese

Leaves from 1 bunch fresh flat-leaf parsley, chopped

2 large eggs

½ teaspoon fresh lemon juice

Pinch of freshly grated nutmeg

Pinch of kosher salt

Pinch of freshly ground black pepper

Onion flowers, for garnish (optional)

the edges down to form a tortellini shape.

Bring a large saucepan of lightly salted water to a boil over medium-high heat. Drop the tortellini into the water and cook until they bob to the surface, 3 to 4 minutes.

Put 4 to 6 tortellini in each shallow serving bowl and pour the hot broth over them. Serve right away. Garnish with onion flowers, if desired.

———

Notes: Bone marrow is found inside the long bones of animals. It's soft, yellowish, and mostly fat and is appreciated by meat eaters the world over for the richness and full flavor it brings to any number of dishes. Beef marrow is the most common in the United States. Ask the butcher to cut the bone marrow bones into 2- to 3-inch lengths.

To char the onion halves, put them cut side up in a small roasting pan and slide them under a preheated broiler. Let them cook until they darken and char around the edges, about 5 minutes. You could also char them by holding them with long-handled tongs over an open gas flame.

Believe it or not, this is one of the first dishes I ever ate in a restaurant. I was on a first date and had ventured outside my little neighborhood. The Thai soup I ordered was a revelation, made exotic with fish sauce and lemongrass, and yet at the end of the day, *tom kha gai* (the official name for this) is a creamy chicken soup ramped up with coconut milk. I don't remember the girl who sat across from me in that little restaurant, but I will never forget the soup!

COCONUT MILK
AND CHICKEN SOUP

In a large soup pot or similar pot, heat the oil over medium-high heat until nearly smoking.

Meanwhile, lightly season the chicken thighs with salt and pepper. Put the chicken in the pot, skin side down, and cook without moving it until the skin starts to separate from the meat, 3 to 4 minutes. Turn the chicken over and sear the other side for 2 to 3 minutes.

Add the stock, coconut milk, mushrooms, lime leaves, lemongrass, lime zest and juice, chiles, ginger, fish sauce, and sugar.

Bring to a boil, reduce the heat, and simmer until the chicken is cooked through and the flavors blend, 40 to 45 minutes, adjusting the heat up or down to maintain the simmer. When done, remove the chicken and shred the meat from the bones. Return the meat to the soup and discard the bones.

Taste and adjust the seasonings—which for this soup usually means a squeeze of lime juice or a drizzle of fish sauce. Serve steaming hot.

———

Note: I like to use palm sugar because it's never refined or bleached and behaves almost exactly like granulated cane sugar. It's rich in nutrients and naturally light brown in color. You can substitute white sugar, but if you can find palm sugar, use it for sure!

SERVES 4 TO 6

3 tablespoons vegetable oil

1 pound boneless, skinless chicken thighs

Kosher salt and freshly ground black pepper

3 cups chicken stock, preferably homemade

1 cup coconut milk

24 oyster mushrooms, thinly sliced

4 lime leaves, or grated zest of 1 lime

1 stalk lemongrass, bottom half only, smashed

Grated zest and juice of 1 lime, plus more juice if necessary

3 or 4 fresh Thai chiles, minced

3 tablespoons grated fresh ginger

2 tablespoons fish sauce, plus more if necessary

2 teaspoons palm sugar (see Note)

Rice porridge—also known as congee—is having a trendy run right now. In fact, it's so trendy, my yoga-teaching hipster wife wants to open a porridge shop! Just about anything goes when it comes to toppings for the thick, creamy soup, although I suggest you skip cheddar-flavored Goldfish crackers (yeah, I tried them once, but only out of late-night desperation). Much better are tasty items such as shredded chicken (or pork if you have some), chopped scallions, grated fresh ginger, and sweet soy sauce.

CHINESE CHICKEN
AND RICE PORRIDGE

In a large soup pot or similar pot, heat the oil over medium-high heat until hot. Put the chicken in the pot, skin side down, and cook without moving it until the skin starts to separate from the meat, 3 to 4 minutes. Turn the chicken over, add the onion, ginger, garlic, and scallion and cook for about 2 minutes. Add the stock and rice.

Bring the soup to a boil, reduce the heat, and simmer until the chicken is cooked through and the flavors blend, 40 to 45 minutes. Adjust the heat up or down to maintain the simmer.

When done, the grains of rice should be swollen and the texture of oatmeal. If the soup is too thick, add a little water or stock.

Lift the chicken from the pot and shred the meat from the bones. Set the meat aside and discard the bones.

Season the soup to taste with salt and white pepper.

Ladle the congee into soup bowls, top each with shredded chicken, and then drizzle with sesame oil, soy sauce, and *kecap manis*, and top with ginger and scallions. Serve hot.

SERVES 4 TO 6

2 tablespoons dark sesame oil

2 bone-in, skin-on chicken thighs

½ yellow onion, diced (about ½ cup)

2 tablespoons grated fresh ginger (1½- to 2-inch knob; you can use a little more if you like), plus more for garnish

6 cloves garlic, smashed

1 scallion, thinly sliced, white and light green parts, plus more for garnish

3 cups chicken stock, preferably homemade

1 generous cup uncooked white rice

Kosher salt and freshly ground white pepper

Dark sesame oil, for garnish

Soy sauce

Kecap manis (Indonesian sweet soy sauce) or your favorite soy sauce, for garnish

I've always thought *borscht* was a horrible word—something you might say when you smell something bad. But despite that, I absolutely, unconditionally love this soup. Hot or cold, it's sweet and tart and minerally, like me. It features beets and dill, both soulful ingredients in my culinary lexicon, and of course its color is one of the most radiant you'll find in a kitchen. When I finish a bowl, my beard has some nice lusty red highlights.

BORSCHT BY BLAIS

In a large soup pot or similar pot, heat the oil over medium heat. When hot, add the onions and caraway seeds and cook, stirring, until the onions begin to soften, 1 to 2 minutes. Add salt to taste and cook, stirring, until the onions are soft and fragrant, 3 to 4 minutes longer.

Stir in the celery and cabbage and add the stock and beet juice. Cook for a few minutes to heat the liquid. When hot, add the potatoes and beets and season to taste with salt and pepper. Stir 1 tablespoon vinegar and 1 tablespoon honey into the soup.

When the soup is simmering, adjust the heat and simmer gently until the potatoes and beets are soft and the soup is full-flavored, about 35 minutes. Taste the soup and adjust if necessary with a bit more vinegar, honey, and/ or salt. Ladle into bowls and serve either warm or chilled, topped with a dollop of sour cream (a nice big dollop, if you are me!), the dill fronds, and the mustard flowers, if using.

———

Note: If you like, use cooked fresh beets in place of canned beets. You will need about half a pound of beets, cooked as you prefer (boiled or roasted), peeled, and diced. In this case, make up the 2 cups of diluted beet juice with vegetable stock.

SERVES 4 TO 6

2 tablespoons extra-virgin olive oil

1 small yellow onion, diced

1 tablespoon crushed caraway seeds

Kosher salt

1 stalk celery, diced

½ small red cabbage, thinly sliced

1 quart vegetable stock, preferably homemade

2 cups beet juice mixed with water or vegetable stock (use the juice from the cans of beets and add enough water or stock to equal 2 cups)

12 small red potatoes or 4 or 5 large ones, diced (no need to peel them)

One 8-ounce can beets (not pickled), drained and diced

Freshly ground black pepper

1 to 2 tablespoons rice wine vinegar

1 to 2 tablespoons honey

Sour cream or fresh soft goat cheese, for topping

¼ cup fresh dill fronds

Small bunch mustard flowers, for garnish (optional)

I admit that my appreciation for the cuisine of New Orleans developed only recently. I used to be the overprivileged, tweezer-sporting "artist" chef who couldn't understand anything as rustic as Creole food, much less Cajun fare. How stupid we are when we're young! (And that wasn't so long ago.)

Gumbo is a commitment. To make it right, the cook has to submit to the process and not rush. Simply stirring a roux as it caramelizes and develops is a labor of love and one that teaches the cook many lessons (see the Notes for more on roux). Its finished color is a drab brown that many would not consider pretty by today's food photography standards, but beauty is truly in the eye of the beholder, and I find dark roux to be a masterpiece. Can you tell that I am a total gumbo convert?

Have fun with gumbo and give it your own personality. Seafood, chicken, vegetarian? Just make sure it comes together slowly and is seasoned to the brink—as much garlic, paprika, and pepper as you can handle. You might want to double this recipe, as the soup only tastes better as it sits. Talk about amazing leftovers. And finally, while you can stir in some filé powder toward the end of cooking, it's traditional in Louisiana to bring filé to the table so those who like it can add even more.

KINDA CLASSIC GUMBO

SERVES 4 TO 6

6 tablespoons vegetable oil

1 pound medium shell-on shrimp (I look for wild American shrimp)

½ cup dark roux (see Notes)

1 yellow onion, diced (about 1 cup)

1 pound andouille sausage, crumbled

1 stalk celery, diced

1 green bell pepper, diced

4 cloves garlic, minced

1 teaspoon cayenne pepper

1 teaspoon sweet paprika

½ teaspoon ground allspice

1½ quarts fish or chicken stock or a mixture, preferably homemade

3 sprigs fresh thyme

1 bay leaf

1 cup lump crabmeat

1 or 2 scallions, sliced, white and light green parts (about ½ cup)

About 2 tablespoons filé powder (optional) (see Notes)

Worcestershire sauce

Tabasco sauce

Kosher salt and freshly ground black pepper

Pickled jalapeños, for topping

In a large soup pot or similar pot, heat the oil over medium-high heat until almost smoking. Add the shrimp and cook for a few minutes, until the shrimp turn pink. Lift the shrimp from the pot and set aside.

Add the roux to the pot and then stir the onions into it. Reduce the heat to medium and continue stirring until the roux darkens a little more and is the consistency of sand at low tide.

Add the sausage and cook, stirring, for 1 minute. Add the celery, bell pepper, and garlic and then stir in the cayenne, paprika, and allspice. When well mixed, add the stock, thyme, and bay leaf.

Bring the gumbo to a boil, reduce the heat, and simmer until the vegetables are tender and the sausage is heated through, about 40 minutes. Skim any fat that rises to the surface of the soup.

Add the crabmeat, scallions, filé powder, if using, and reserved shrimp and cook over medium heat until heated through, 5 to 8 minutes. Season to taste with Worcestershire and Tabasco. Taste and season with salt and pepper.

Ladle the gumbo into soup bowls and serve topped with pickled jalapeños. Serve hot, and don't forget the napkins!

Notes: To make roux, begin with equal amounts of vegetable oil (such as canola or corn) and flour. It's best to start with at least 1 cup of oil and 1 cup of flour, as smaller amounts can be tricky to work with. Heat the oil in a deep skillet over medium heat until hot (I like to use a cast-iron skillet). Gradually add the flour, whisking and stirring constantly to ensure the two ingredients mix and the flour is lump-free. Lower the heat to low and continue cooking, stirring often, for about 30 minutes, or until the color is uniformly light brown. Cook the roux for about 15 minutes longer, or until the color darkens further and the aroma is nutty. The roux will be thick. It's now ready for gumbo!

Filé powder is made from finely ground sassafras leaves. It's sometimes called gumbo powder or gumbo seasoning because it's used to flavor and thicken traditional gumbo.

PASTA

I've always loved the romance of Italy and its food. Perfect pasta, made with nothing more than flour and water (and sometimes egg), is mind-blowing. And pasta is the perfect go-to meal when you don't have much time; you can always throw together a really good pasta dish.

These are some of my faves. Family tested and with traces of Southern California in every bite—sort of Cal-Italian. My restaurant Juniper and Ivy is on the edge of San Diego's robust Little Italy neighborhood, and a good number of our dishes reflect that influence. The Cal part of the equation is found in whole-grain pastas and the fresh, ripe veggies tossed with them. My roots are East Coast, but my kitchen is firmly in the Golden State, and while I often crave the classic red-sauce pastas of my Long Island childhood, I can't resist the sunny, veg-driven pastas I cook here.

I should be ashamed to include a dish in this book that translates to "in the style of the whore," but because my version is green, it's a little more like "in the style of a casual floozy." Clearly, I'll need an Italian-American dictionary to translate it properly. But whatever it's called, this is loaded with big, salty, fishy, garlicky, acidic flavors. You won't be kissing your wife or husband for a while after you eat this—not even your mother—but let's face it, it's fun to be a little promiscuous with ingredients to make a big, bold, totally delicious meal. I like to make this with bucatini, those long, narrow, hollow tubes of pasta that work so well with chunky sauces.

BUCATINI PUTTANESCA

Bring a large pot of salted water to a boil. Add the pasta and cook until it is nearly al dente, 5 to 8 minutes. Reserve ½ cup of the pasta cooking water and drain the pasta.

Put the zucchini, spinach, and basil in a blender or, if you're old-world, a mortar. Drizzle with about 1 teaspoon of the olive oil and pulse or use the pestle to pound the vegetables to a paste. Set aside.

In a large sauté pan, heat ¼ cup of the oil over medium heat. Add the anchovies and capers and cook, stirring, until the capers begin to brown, 2 to 3 minutes. Add the remaining oil, the olives, garlic, scallions, and red pepper flakes and cook, stirring, until the garlic is soft and fragrant, 2 to 3 minutes more. Your kitchen should be filled with aroma at this point.

Add the reserved zucchini-spinach paste and stir to mix. Transfer the mixture to the bowl of a food processor fitted with the metal blade and pulse 2 or 3 times until blended but still a little chunky.

Add the pasta and toss with the sauce until thoroughly coated. Add some of the reserved pasta water, if the pasta seems dry. Squeeze the lemon juice over the pasta and season to taste with salt. Serve hot.

SERVES 4

Kosher salt

1 pound dry bucatini

2 small zucchini, grated

2 cups loosely packed spinach leaves

½ cup loosely packed fresh basil leaves

½ cup extra-virgin olive oil

3 or 4 anchovy filets (depending on how much you like anchovies)

¼ cup drained capers

1 cup pitted green olives, thinly sliced

8 cloves green garlic, peeled and cut into ⅛-inch-thick slices, or 4 cloves garlic, sliced

⅓ cup thinly sliced scallions, white and light green parts only

1 teaspoon crushed red pepper flakes

½ lemon

Let's be honest, *gnudi* is fun to say (it's a silent "g"). Serve them with cockles and you're guaranteed a few laughs. But seriously, homemade gnudi can take up to three days to dry, and we don't have time for that here! Wringing the liquid from the ricotta will expedite the matter exponentially. When you cook the chilled, dumpling-like pieces of pasta, use a gentle hand. Sorrel accentuates the tart, lemony flavor of this elegant dish, so if you can find it, use it.

GNUDI AND
BROWN BUTTER

Line a baking sheet with parchment paper and evenly spread about three-quarters of the semolina on the sheet.

Wrap the ricotta in a double thickness of cheesecloth and squeeze gently but firmly to release as much moisture as possible. Transfer the ricotta to a mixing bowl and grate 1 ounce of the Parmesan over it. Add 1 teaspoon salt and stir to combine.

Spoon the cheese into a disposable piping bag or sturdy plastic bag. Cut a large opening that is about 1¼ inches across in the tip of the bag or corner of the plastic bag. Pipe the cheese onto the bed of semolina on the baking sheet into 3 or 4 straight lines, each about ½ inch wide, and leaving 1 to 2 inches between them.

Using kitchen shears, carefully snip each strip all along its length, at about 1½-inch intervals. You now have made gnudi! Dust the gnudi with the reserved semolina.

Refrigerate the gnudi for at least 8 hours or preferably overnight. Do not cover them; let them air-dry.

Bring a large pot of generously salted water to a boil. Slip some of the gnudi into the pot and cook, gently shaking the pot, until they bob to the surface, about 2 minutes. Work in batches so as not to crowd the pot, and avoid overcooking or the gnudi will fall apart. Using a slotted spoon, quickly transfer the gnudi to a dry plate.

Heat a large skillet over medium heat and, when hot, melt the butter. When it bubbles, let it cook without stirring for 2 to 3 minutes to allow the moisture to evaporate. Cook for a few minutes longer, stirring constantly, until the butter darkens in color and its fragrance is nutty. Remove from the heat.

Toss the gnudi in the butter, add the sage and sorrel, and season to taste with salt. Divide the gnudi among plates and finely grate the remaining ½ ounce Parmesan over it. Season with lemon juice and finish with a drizzle of olive oil and a little pepper.

Note: Sorrel leaves are pretty, with a variegated pattern and triangular shape. Yet it's their tart-sour flavor that attracts cooks. You've most likely heard of sorrel soup, a great favorite in France. I fully admit that sorrel can be hard to find, although you might have good luck at farmer's markets and places like Whole Foods. If you can't find it, substitute baby spinach leaves and maybe spritz a little more lemon juice over the pasta, if you like.

SERVES 4

- 1 pound semolina flour
- 1 pound ricotta cheese
- About 1½ ounces Parmesan cheese
- Kosher salt
- 3 tablespoons good-quality unsalted butter, cut into chunks
- Small handful of fresh white or common sage, chopped
- 1 tablespoon torn sorrel leaves or baby spinach (see Note)
- 1 lemon, halved
- Extra-virgin olive oil
- Freshly ground black pepper

Curiously, this dish seems very French, which to me means that it is thoughtful and elegant. I trained in French cuisine and have a good handle on that magnificent repertoire. And yet, the earthiness of the buckwheat mixed with the oceanic flavor of crab makes this a "new" rendition of surf and earth. Caviar would be a posh yet worthy addition and would elevate its elegance and luxury even as it enhances the salty flavors of the ocean. While not absolutely necessary, fresh tagliatelle makes this dish even better—so use it if you can.

BUCKWHEAT TAGLIATELLE
WITH CRABMEAT

SERVES 4

Kosher salt

1 pound fresh buckwheat or 12 ounces dry tagliatelle (or fettuccine)

1 cup (2 sticks) unsalted butter, at room temperature

Grated zest of 2 lemons

1 bunch fresh shiso leaves, chopped (see Note)

2 tablespoons extra-virgin olive oil, plus more for drizzling

½ yellow onion, minced (about ½ cup)

2 cloves garlic, minced

¼ cup chicken or vegetable stock, preferably homemade

½ pound lump crabmeat

Freshly ground black pepper

½ cup Seasoned Bread Crumbs (page 217)

2 jalapeños, seeded and finely diced

Juice of 1 or 2 lemons

Bring a large pot of salted water to a boil over medium-high heat. Add the pasta and cook according to the package instructions. Reserve about ¼ cup of the pasta cooking water and drain the pasta.

In the bowl of a food processor fitted with a metal blade, combine the butter, lemon zest, and shiso leaves and pulse until the mixture is blended. Scrape the butter into a small bowl and set aside.

Heat a large sauté pan over medium heat. Add the olive oil and, when hot, add the onions and garlic and cook, stirring, until the onions are softened and fragrant, about 2 minutes. Add the stock, bring it to a gentle boil, and deglaze the pan by scraping up the browned bits sticking to the bottom. Add 1 to 2 table-spoons of the shiso butter and stir to mix and incorporate. Add more if desired (and save the rest for another day). Gently stir in the crabmeat and let it heat gently just until hot.

With the pan still set over the heat, use a slotted spoon to transfer the cooked pasta to the pan, and toss gently until coated with the sauce. Add a little pasta water if necessary to thin and extend the sauce. The noodles should be coated in sauce, not swimming in it.

Season with salt and pepper to taste and sprinkle the bread crumbs and jalapeños over the pasta. Drizzle with olive oil and the lemon juice and serve immediately.

———————

Note: Shiso leaves (also called perilla) are used throughout Asia as a seasoning. Their flavor is at once citrusy, herby, and minty, which is not surprising since shiso is part of the mint family. Their jagged leaves can be green or purplish. If you can't find shiso, substitute mild fresh mint or fresh basil.

Broccoli fascinates me. Admittedly, saying so makes me an absolute food nerd (although, if not me, who?). But I approach it with the technical precision I usually reserve for meat. Its many parts require different cooking methods. For this recipe, I shave the florets of their fuzziness or "hair" just like I shave my face. I use a small, sharp knife (not a razor) that I run over the florets so that they flake. I use the flakes to coat the noodles. The broccoli gives the dish the appearance of pesto but with far less work. It's green and herbaceous, and I'm pretty sure whole wheat anything is healthy, right?

WHOLE WHEAT
SPAGHETTINI AND PESTO

SERVES 4

Kosher salt

1 pound dry whole wheat spaghettini

5 tablespoons extra-virgin olive oil

Florets from 2 heads broccoli, shaved into crumbs

2 tablespoons minced yellow onion

2 cloves garlic, minced

1 teaspoon crushed red pepper flakes

1 cup chopped flat-leaf parsley

6 fresh basil leaves

¼ cup pine nuts, toasted (see Note)

Grated zest and juice of 1 lemon

Kosher salt and freshly ground black pepper

5 tablespoons freshly grated pecorino cheese

Bring a large pot of salted water to a boil. Add the pasta and cook according to the package instructions until al dente. Drain the pasta, reserving 2 to 3 tablespoons of the pasta cooking water.

In a large skillet, heat 2½ tablespoons of the oil over medium heat and, when hot, add the broccoli crumbs, onion, garlic, and red pepper flakes. Cook, stirring, until fragrant, about 1 minute. Add the parsley, basil leaves, and pine nuts and stir to incorporate.

Remove the skillet from the heat. Add the drained spaghetti and toss to coat. Season with the lemon zest and juice and salt and pepper to taste. Sprinkle the cheese over the pasta and drizzle with the remaining 2½ tablespoons olive oil. Serve hot.

Note: To toast pine nuts, spread them in a small, dry frying pan and toast over medium heat, stirring, for 2 to 3 minutes, until they turn golden brown. The coloring may not be even, but that's okay. Take care that they don't burn. Slide onto a plate to halt the cooking.

I created this dish through pure observation: like with like. When I see seashell pasta, naturally I want to pair it with a shelled sea creature. Being me, I went with conch and uni (sea urchin), both outstanding eats. Clams, abalone, and even shrimp make excellent substitutes.

The sauce essentially is a riff on white clam sauce, one of my absolute favorites, and something I grew up requesting for my birthday dinners. That boy, a chubby twelve-year-old Blais, wouldn't have been too keen on either uni or conch, but the grown-up Blais can assure you there are no better two ingredients to translate the flavors of the sea.

SHELLS WITH
UNI AND CONCH

Bring a large pot of salted water to a boil. Add the pasta and cook according to the package instructions.

In the bowl of a food processor fitted with a metal blade, combine half of the uni, the butter, half of the onion, and the oregano. Pulse until the mixture is blended. Scrape the butter into a small bowl and set aside.

Heat a large sauté pan over medium heat. When hot, add the olive oil. Add the garlic and the remaining onion and cook, stirring, until the garlic softens and is fragrant, about 2 minutes. Add the wine, bring to a rapid simmer, and cook for 6 to 8 minutes, until the liquid is almost fully reduced.

Add the clam juice and ¼ cup of the uni butter. Bring to a simmer and cook until the liquid is reduced by half, about 10 minutes. Stir the conch into the sauce and cook for 5 to 7 minutes longer.

Using a slotted spoon, transfer the pasta to the pan, add the remaining uni butter, and toss over medium heat to coat the pasta and allow the butter to melt.

Season to taste with salt and pepper. Serve immediately, topped with the bread crumbs and a drizzle of olive oil.

———

Note: Fresh uni, which is the Japanese name for the meat of sea urchins, is often sold in trays, usually weighing 40 grams (about 1½ ounces) or 120 grams (about 4 ounces). If you can't find uni trays at your local seafood market, buy any sashimi tray—a container of fresh, raw seafood. It will work in this recipe. Freshness and local-ness, my friends, are key here.

SERVES 4

Kosher salt

1 pound dry small pasta shells

4 ounces local uni (one 120-gram or three 40-gram trays) (see Note)

1 cup (2 sticks) unsalted butter, at room temperature

1 white onion, minced (about 1 cup)

2 teaspoons dried oregano

2 tablespoons extra-virgin olive oil, plus more for drizzling

2 cloves garlic, minced

½ cup white wine

2 cups bottled clam juice

1 pound raw conch or clams, finely diced

Freshly ground black pepper

½ cup Seasoned Bread Crumbs (page 217)

Radiatore translates to . . . tiny little radiators? Who wouldn't love this shape? I know I do! (In my spare time, I'm working on tiny little steam iron–shaped pasta.) Radiatore's coils and its density give it excellent cling-ability so that the little ridges grab hold of and trap the meaty sauce. Rabbit? Sure, it kind of tastes like chicken—and you have my permission to substitute ground or shredded chicken here. Still, rabbit opens up a much bigger dinner table discussion and scores points with the judges for originality.

RADIATORE BOLOGNESE

In a large pot, heat the oil over medium-high heat. Add the onions, celery, and carrots and cook, stirring, until the onions are translucent and fragrant, about 5 minutes. Add the rabbit and pancetta and cook, stirring to prevent sticking, for 5 minutes longer.

Bring a large pot of salted water to a boil.

Meanwhile, stir the tomato paste into the rabbit mixture and allow it to almost burn in the pan. Add the wine and stir with a wooden spoon, scraping up any bits sticking to the pot. Add 2 cups of the stock and stir well. Reduce the heat to medium-low and simmer gently, stirring often, until the flavors meld, 10 to 12 minutes. Season to taste with salt.

Cook the pasta in the boiling water according to the package directions. Drain and transfer the pasta to the pot with the rabbit sauce. Add as much of the remaining 1 cup stock to thin the sauce to the desired consistency and toss to coat the pasta thoroughly, then add the butter. Stir to distribute the melting butter evenly. Serve immediately, topped with the Parmesan and bread crumbs.

SERVES 4

2 tablespoons extra-virgin olive oil

1 yellow onion, finely chopped (about 1 cup)

2 stalks celery, finely chopped (about ¾ cup)

1 carrot, peeled and finely chopped (about ½ cup)

1 pound ground or cooked and shredded rabbit, white meat only

⅓ cup finely chopped pancetta

Kosher salt

2 tablespoons tomato paste

½ cup red wine

3 cups chicken stock, preferably homemade

1 pound dry radiatore

2 tablespoons good-quality unsalted butter

About ½ cup freshly grated Parmesan cheese, or to taste

1 cup Seasoned Bread Crumbs (page 217)

When you combine bone marrow and marinara, you get bone marrownara! Head to your local butcher or good meat counter and ask for marrow or soup bones—and then ask the butcher to chop them for you. This saves a lot of time and hassle and most butchers don't mind. Here I use ricotta instead of the more expected bread crumbs to make the meatballs light and fluffy. I sprinkle bread crumbs over the finished dish just before serving, so they are not totally abandoned.

SPAGHETTI AND BONE
MARROWNARA MEATBALLS

SERVES 4

1 yellow onion, diced (about 1 cup)

4 cloves garlic, minced

1 tablespoon crushed red pepper flakes

2 tablespoons tomato paste

One 32-ounce can whole tomatoes and their juices

¼ cup red wine

1 cup ricotta cheese

8 ounces ground pork

8 ounces ground beef

3 tablespoons chopped fresh basil

2 teaspoons chopped fresh oregano

2 teaspoons chopped fresh sage

1 tablespoon chopped fresh rosemary

1 tablespoon finely chopped fresh flat-leaf parsley

Kosher salt and freshly ground black pepper

3 to 4 tablespoons extra-virgin olive oil

¼ cup chopped bone marrow

12 ounces dry spaghetti

1 cup plain bread crumbs, toasted

About ¼ cup grated Parmesan cheese

In a large pot, mix the onion, garlic, and red pepper flakes. Cook, stirring, over medium-high heat until the onions are translucent and fragrant, 3 to 4 minutes. Remove half of the contents from the pot and let cool to lukewarm. Transfer to a lidded container and refrigerate to cool completely. Meanwhile, add the tomato paste to the pot with the remaining onions and cook, stirring, until the natural sugars in the paste begin to caramelize and it is fragrant, about 3 minutes. Add the canned tomatoes and cook, stirring constantly and scraping the bottom of the pot to make sure nothing burns, until heated through.

Add the wine and cook over medium-high heat for about 5 minutes to give the alcohol in the wine a chance to evaporate. Use a wooden spoon to stir and scrape up any bits that might stick to the bottom of the pan. Reduce the heat to medium-low and simmer, stirring occasionally to ensure the sauce does not burn, for about 18 minutes longer.

In a medium mixing bowl, stir the ricotta with the refrigerated onion-garlic mixture. Add the ground pork, ground beef, basil, oregano, sage, and rosemary. Gently mix the meat with your hands and, when just combined, add the

parsley and season to taste with salt and pepper. Mix thoroughly, but take care not to overmix. (If you handle the meat too much, the fat will emulsify from the heat of your hands and the meatballs will be dense and leaden.) Shape the meat into meatballs the size of Ping-Pong balls.

In a large sauté pan, heat 3 tablespoons of the oil over medium-high heat. Working in batches so as not to crowd the pan and adding a little more oil as needed, sear the meatballs lightly on all sides until they begin to brown. They will not be fully cooked. Transfer the meatballs to the tomato sauce, add the bone marrow, and simmer the sauce over low heat for about 20 minutes to finish cooking the meatballs and allow the bone marrow to render its fat. Make sure to add any accumulated fat from the meatballs to this sauce!

While the meatballs and sauce are cooking, bring a large pot of salted water to a boil and cook the pasta according to the package directions. Drain the pasta and add it to the sauce and meatballs. Toss well and serve immediately, garnished with the bread crumbs and Parmesan cheese.

FISH AND SEAFOOD

At the end of the day, fish cookery comes down to a hot pan. Don't be afraid to let it get really hot. This means that any oil will be at its smoking point, so when the fish hits the scorching surface it can be moved around without sticking. Now you've done your job.

A lot of home cooks don't cook much fish, no matter how often they order it when dining out. They're wary of cooking it at home. When I trained to be a chef at the CIA, I was a student-teacher in the fish department, and since then I've cooked just about every kind of fish in the sea. Believe me, the recipes in this chapter are foolproof. They fall into the meaty, substantial category of fish and seafood cooking. No fragile fillet of sole that needs a tender hand. These are designed to go with a gutsy red wine, as opposed to the dishes in the Starters chapter, which, being more delicate, call for white wine.

You could call this an entry-level fish dish—it's that easy. But beyond its simplicity, the fatty lusciousness of sea bass contrasts gorgeously with the crunch of bok choy and the spiciness of the sauce spiked with ginger beer.

SEA BASS WITH GINGER
BEER AND BOK CHOY

Trim the bok choy and cut out any thick stems. Rinse under cool, running water and shake most of the water from the leaves.

Pour water into a large, deep skillet to a depth of 2 inches or so and season lightly with salt. Put a steamer basket over the water and bring to a boil over high heat. Put the bok choy leaves (they don't have to be dry) in the skillet, salt lightly, cover the pan, and reduce the heat to medium. Steam the bok choy until the leaves wilt, 7 to 9 minutes. Remove the lid from the skillet and continue cooking for about 1 minute to evaporate any excess water clinging to the leaves (there will be some water in the pan, but no worries).

Meanwhile, season the sea bass fillets on both sides with salt and pepper.

In a large sauté pan, heat the sesame oil with 1 tablespoon of the butter over medium-high heat. When hot, add the fillets and cook until golden brown and cooked through, 4 to 5 minutes per side. Remove the fillets from the heat, set aside on a plate, and cover with aluminum foil to keep warm.

Pour the ginger beer into the sauté pan (after you've taken a few nips yourself) and stir to mix with the pan juices. Bring to a boil over high heat, reduce the heat a little, and simmer until the beer evaporates, leaving a thickish, slightly oozy glaze in the pan, 8 to 10 minutes. As the pan sauce simmers, stir it with a wooden spoon to scrape any browned bits from the bottom of the pan.

Add the grated ginger and lime juice to the pan and swirl to mix. Add the remaining 3 table-spoons butter and stir until the pan sauce is smooth and thick.

Serve the fillets on top of the wilted bok choy. Spoon a little sauce over the fish and garnish with the cilantro, if desired.

Note: Chilean sea bass is pretty expensive and rare. If you can't find it or would rather use another fish, try black cod (also called Alaskan sablefish). It's more affordable and plentiful in our oceans, and it has a similar buttery texture and mild but delicious flavor as sea bass. I always check with the Seafood Watch app, which is run by the greatly respected Monterey Bay Aquarium. This keeps me up to date with what fish are currently sustainable and good choices.

SERVES 4

1 bunch bok choy (about 1 pound)

Kosher salt

4 Chilean sea bass fillets (6 to 8 ounces each) (see Note)

Freshly ground black pepper

1 tablespoon dark sesame oil

4 tablespoons (½ stick) unsalted butter

One 12-ounce bottle ginger beer

1-inch knob fresh ginger, peeled and grated

Juice of 1 lime

2 to 3 tablespoons chopped fresh cilantro, or 2 lime leaves, sliced (optional)

I'm sort of obsessed with the gastronomic classics, and beef Wellington is a star in that firmament. To make it, beef tenderloin is coated with mushroom duxelles and then encased in buttery puff pastry. Um . . . *yum*! Tuna is just as lean as beef tenderloin and visually more of a showstopper, so a quick swap transports this classic to the future. To make it even more special, fold some chicken liver or foie gras mousse into the chilled mushrooms. Talk about luxury.

TUNA WELLINGTON

SERVES 6

2 tablespoons unsalted butter

1 tablespoon minced yellow onion

2 cloves garlic, minced

2½ quarts (about 5 pints) white button mushrooms, stemmed and finely chopped

Kosher salt and freshly ground black pepper

1 to 2 tablespoons chopped fresh flat-leaf parsley

1 sprig fresh thyme

1 ahi tuna tenderloin (4 to 5 pounds)

1 to 2 teaspoons curry powder

1 sheet frozen puff pastry, thawed

In a large sauté pan, heat the butter over medium-high heat, and when it melts and bubbles, add the onion and garlic and cook, stirring, for about 1 minute. Lower the heat a little to keep the garlic from burning. Add the mushrooms and cook, stirring, until they soften, 10 to 12 minutes. Season to taste with salt and pepper and continue cooking until the mushrooms exude their moisture, 3 to 5 minutes.

Add the parsley and thyme to the mushrooms, stir gently, and cook for a few minutes longer. Remove the pan from the heat and let cool. When at room temperature, chill the mushrooms for at least 1 hour.

Season both sides of the tuna with the curry powder and salt and pepper. Refrigerate the tuna until cold, at least 1 hour.

Preheat the oven to 400°F.

Lay the puff pastry on a work surface and, using the tines of a fork or a small, sharp knife, prick the pastry all over to dock it. This will keep it from bubbling during baking. If you want to make the pastry look like it does in the picture on the opposite page, use a small ring mold or even a metal bottle cap to make overlapping, shingled curved indents to resemble fish scales. This works best if the pastry is still frozen.

Put the chilled tuna tenderloin in the center of the pastry. Top the tuna with the chilled mushroom mixture. Fold the pastry over and around the tuna to enclose it completely and securely.

Transfer the wrapped tuna to a shallow roasting pan and bake for 20 to 25 minutes, until the pastry is golden brown. The wrapped tuna will be medium-rare.

Slice the Wellington and serve it with your favorite mashed potatoes or roasted vegetables.

Clearly I'm a big fan of nineties hip-hop and have offered these clams in restaurants with the tag, "Ain't nothin' to shuck with!" Other than its verbal cleverness, this refers to the power of the oceans, too. Clams and other mollusks thrive despite the ocean's might—or because of it? Small and unassuming, but producing a powerhouse stock the minute their shells are opened. Rustle up some french fries or crusty bread for soppin' it up!

WU-TANG CLAMS

In a deep pot with a lid, heat the sesame oil over medium-high heat and, when hot, add the scallions, garlic, and ginger. Cook, stirring and taking care not to burn the garlic, for 1 to 2 minutes. Add the sausage and bok choy and cook, stirring, until the bok choy starts to wilt, 1 to 2 minutes.

Add the clams and wine, scraping up any bits sticking to the bottom of the pan. Add the butter, cover the pot, and cook, shaking the pan now and then, until the clams open, 5 to 6 minutes.

Remove the pot from the heat and add the cilantro, a drizzle of soy sauce, the sambal, and the lemon juice. Toss a few times and then turn the clams out of the pot into a serving dish. Serve with crusty bread for sopping up the juices.

───────

Note: Chinese sausages are commonly made from pork, although you will find duck and chicken sausages, too, at most Asian markets. They can be fresh or smoked and are often known by their Cantonese name, *lap cheong.* They are mild sausages, and you can substitute your favorite mild pork sausage for the sausages here.

SERVES 4 TO 6

1 tablespoon dark sesame oil

2 or 3 scallions, sliced, white and light green parts only

2 cloves garlic, minced

1-inch knob fresh ginger, peeled and chopped

2 fresh Chinese pork sausages, chopped (see Note)

1 bunch bok choy, stems trimmed and leaves rinsed with some water left clinging to them

48 to 60 littleneck clams, scrubbed

3 to 4 tablespoons Chinese cooking wine or sherry

½ cup (1 stick) unsalted butter, cut into pieces

2 tablespoons chopped fresh cilantro

1 to 2 teaspoons soy sauce

About 2 teaspoons sambal or another Asian chili sauce

Juice of ½ lemon

Crusty bread, for serving

Eating shrimp in its shell has an animalistic quality that makes this a messy pig of a dish that's both spicy and creamy—and full of character. I won't call it authentic New Orleans fare, because I'm no expert on that cuisine, but I will call it easy and irresistibly craveable! So cover the table with newspapers or wax paper, open the beer, and go for it!

BARBECUED SHRIMP

In a glass, ceramic, or other nonreactive bowl, mix the oil with the Cajun spices. Put the shrimp in the bowl and toss or stir around to coat with the mixture. Its consistency will be between a marinade and a rub. Cover and refrigerate for at least 1 hour but not much longer than 1 hour and 30 minutes.

In a small bowl, mix the 4 tablespoons of room-temperature butter with the garlic. Mash the garlic butter a few times to make sure to distribute the garlic evenly, and set aside at room temperature.

Preheat the oven to 425°F.

Heat a large skillet (I recommend a cast-iron skillet if possible) over medium-high heat until very hot. Lift the shrimp from the marinade and drop them directly into the skillet. (The oil on the shrimp makes it unnecessary to oil the skillet.) Cook the shrimp, stirring gently and turning a few times, until they turn bright pink, 3 to 4 minutes.

Pour a good splash of beer into the pan and stir to scrape up any browned bits from the bottom of the pan. Transfer the shrimp and the pan liquid to a bowl.

Add the Worcestershire sauce to the hot pan and enough of the remaining chilled butter to make a thick, smooth glaze. Pour this over the shrimp and stir to coat the shrimp.

Meanwhile, butter the baguettes with the garlic butter and arrange, buttered sides up, on a shallow baking tray. Toast in the hot oven for 3 to 5 minutes, until the butter melts and the bread starts to brown and turn crispy around the edges.

Put the toasted baguettes on a warm platter and pour the shrimp and any accumulated liquid over the baguettes. Sprinkle with the parsley and shout *"Bam!"*

SERVES 4

3 tablespoons extra-virgin olive oil

2 tablespoons Cajun seasoning (your favorite brand)

1 pound large shrimp, heads on and in the shell

6 to 7 tablespoons unsalted butter, 4 tablespoons at room temperature and the remaining chilled

1 clove garlic, finely chopped

2 to 3 tablespoons beer (whatever you're drinking)

3 tablespoons Worcestershire sauce

Four 8- to 10-inch baguettes, split open

About 1 tablespoon chopped fresh flat-leaf parsley

Of course this is best if you catch the trout yourself—and of course any fresh trout will do just fine (btw, golden trout are a subspecies of rainbows). If you can catch a golden trout in an alpine river and then cook it outdoors, this dish is perfect for more reasons than the food. But the flavors are perfect whether you're indoors or out.

GOLDEN TROUT ON
CEDAR WITH CAMPFIRE BAKED BEANS

Season the trout with salt and pepper. Sandwich 2 slices of bacon between 2 of the fillets, and the other 2 bacon slices between the remaining fillets. Put the prepared fish on the soaked cedar plank.

Prepare a gas or charcoal grill so that the heating element or coals are medium-hot.

Grill the trout on the plank for 15 to 17 minutes, until the bacon is cooked and the trout is just cooked through. Remove from the grill and transfer from the plank to a warm platter.

In a skillet, melt the butter over medium heat and cook without stirring to give the moisture time to evaporate, about 2 minutes. Continue cooking, stirring, until the butter darkens and smells nutty, 3 to 4 minutes.

Add the nuts, dill, capers, and lemon juice to the butter and stir. Brush on or pour the mixture over the fish so that it's shiny and delicious. Serve the fish with the baked beans.

SERVES 4

4 golden trout or brook trout fillets or whole fish

Kosher salt and freshly ground black pepper

4 slices bacon

Cedar plank (or similar wood plank made for cooking), soaked in water

2 tablespoons unsalted butter

¼ cup chopped walnuts, pecans, or almonds

2 tablespoons chopped fresh dill

1 tablespoon drained capers

Squeeze of fresh lemon juice

Campfire Baked Beans (page 210)

Fish tails don't get much respect. Time to change that! Treat a salmon tail as a tougher cut of meat and cook it a little longer than usual, or braise it as I do here. Because it's cooked on the bone, the salmon takes on the meaty quality I love, which is why I sometimes team this with lentils for a riff on pork and beans.

SALMON TAIL WITH
BACON AND LENTILS

Fill a large bowl with about 10 cups of water (you want to soak the lentils in five times more water than their volume). Add the lentils and let them soak for 8 to 10 hours or overnight.

Preheat the oven to 350°F.

Set a deep saucepan over medium-high heat. When hot, add the carrots, onion, and bacon and cook, stirring, for about 5 minutes or until the onion starts to soften and the bacon renders its fat and starts to cook.

Drain the lentils and add them to the pan. Add the mustard and vinegar, stir to mix, and season to taste with salt. Stir in the curry powder. Set aside, covered, to keep warm.

Season the salmon tail with salt and pepper.

In an oven-safe skillet large enough to hold the salmon tail, melt the butter over medium heat. When bubbling, add the salmon to the pan

and cook for 2 to 3 minutes. Turn the salmon over and cook for 2 to 3 minutes on the other side. Transfer the skillet to the oven and cook the salmon for about 10 minutes longer or until cooked through. And you're done. (I like to cook this in a wood-burning oven, but you may not have one.)

Slice the salmon and serve with the lentils.

———

Note: Salmon tails may not sound familiar when you think of salmon, but they are mighty tasty and often are less expensive than other cuts of salmon. Ask the fishmonger to cut the tail for you. And if there is not a fishmonger handy and you can't find the tails, use salmon fillets. They'll work. Watch them closely; they'll need 3 to 4 minutes on each side in the skillet. That's it. No oven for them.

SERVES 4

2 cups Puy lentils

1 carrot, chopped (about ¼ cup)

1 small yellow onion, chopped

½ cup chopped bacon (about 8 ounces)

1 tablespoon good mustard, such as Dijon or a full-flavored mustard from your favorite specialty store

1 tablespoon malt vinegar

Kosher salt

1 to 2 teaspoons Jamaican curry powder

Two 12-ounce salmon tail fillets or salmon fillets (see Note)

Freshly ground black pepper

2 tablespoons unsalted butter (I like to use clarified butter)

CHICKEN, TURKEY, DUCK, GOOSE, SQUAB (AND RABBIT)

Yes, all the recipes here can be made with chicken, so don't panic when you see duck and squab. Substitute chicken, #apopularbird. Still, I can't write a book about chicken alone, as beloved as it may be, and so I have included recipes for turkey, goose, duck, and squab as well. You can find these birds in many supermarkets and specialty shops, or you may have to preorder them, but that's no big deal. A small price for such succulent meat and glorious flavors.

Funny thing about chicken: The boneless, skinless chicken breasts Americans consume week in and week out are tricky to cook. They're as temperamental as lobster tail: Underdone chicken freaks people out; overdone is dry and stringy. Are your chicken breasts just about perfect? If so, you're more than ready for duck, squab, and goose. Oh! I also have a recipe for rabbit. Rabbits may not have feathers, but they "taste like chicken."

Copious amounts of garlic and acid (lemon juice, vinegar, and capers here) figure large in my cooking. This may sound aggressive or overly masculine—neither of which especially describes me—but I believe learning how to use both liberally is a sign of a confident cook. These vibrant ingredients wake up just about everything, and although they're not needed in every dish, a drop here and there is almost always beneficial. And garlic? Vampire repellant, duh. . . .

CHICKEN WITH GARLIC
AND ROSEMARY

In a large pot, melt the butter over medium-low heat and cook until it begins to brown and gives off a nutty fragrance. Add the garlic, carrots, and onions and cook, stirring, until the vegetables begin to brown slightly, 5 to 6 minutes.

Meanwhile, lightly season the chicken with salt and pepper. Add to the pot along with the stock, raise the heat to medium-high, and bring to a boil. Skim off any foam that rises to the surface, reduce the heat to medium-low, and simmer until the chicken is cooked through, about 1 hour.

Add the chiles, rosemary, capers, lemon juice, and vinegar to the stew and cook for 2 to 3 minutes to give the flavors time to blend.

Put a chicken thigh in each shallow bowl. Ladle the broth over the chicken and serve piping-hot, drizzled with chili oil.

———

Notes: Calabrian chiles are medium-size chiles that are allowed to turn dark red on the vine and provide fruity, mild heat to any number of dishes, including pizzas, pastas, stews, and soups. They are available fresh and dried. While they are great for infusing oils at home, you can also buy Calabrian chili oil.

I like to use chicken thighs for this recipe, but a whole chicken (see photo) works just as well. Put the seasoned bird in a deep skillet and follow the recipe as written. A whole chicken will need 20 to 30 minutes longer to cook than the thighs. Either way, a winner!

SERVES 4

2 tablespoons unsalted butter

Cloves from 1 head garlic
(10 to 12, usually), thinly shaved

2 or 3 carrots, chopped
(about 1 cup)

1 yellow onion, chopped
(about 1 cup)

4 bone-in, skin-on chicken thighs

Kosher salt and freshly
ground black pepper

1 quart chicken stock, preferably
homemade

3 fresh Calabrian chiles,
chopped (see Notes)

5 sprigs fresh rosemary

2 tablespoons drained capers

Juice of 1 lemon

Generous splash of white wine
vinegar

1 tablespoon Calabrian chili oil
(see Notes)

Who poaches chicken anyhow? Well, I do . . . and so will you. The salad combines some of my favorite aromatics for a refreshing, satiating meal. Don't be shy with the fish sauce. You'll be surprised how much oomph a little rotten fish provides. And once the chicken is poached, save the poaching liquid to drink or serve it as an exciting new take on chicken soup.

VIETNAMESE-STYLE
CHICKEN NOODLE SALAD

Fill a large pot about three-quarters full with cold water. Bring it to a boil over high heat, add the rice noodles, and cook until al dente, 3 to 4 minutes. Drain and shock them to stop the cooking by dunking them in a large bowl filled with ice and cold water. Drain the noodles and set aside.

In a large pot, combine the chicken stock with the lemongrass, ginger, garlic, and star anise and bring to a boil over medium-high heat.

Meanwhile, season the chicken with salt. When the stock boils, reduce the heat so it simmers. Add the chicken and poach just until cooked through, 15 to 18 minutes. Remove the chicken from the poaching liquid and set aside. (Reserve the poaching liquid for another meal or to drink as a soup.)

In a lidded glass jar (I like to use a Mason jar) or similar container, combine the vinegar with the oil. Add the cilantro, scallions, jalapeño, ginger, garlic, sriracha, lime juice, and fish sauce. Shake to mix.

Put the noodles in a mixing bowl (they can be cool or room temperature; either way is fine), add the torn lettuce leaves, and toss to mix. Dress with the vinaigrette and serve the noodles with the chicken.

SERVES 4

1 pound dry rice noodles

3 quarts chicken stock, preferably homemade

1 stalk lemongrass, trimmed and coarsely chopped

1½- to 2-inch knob fresh ginger, peeled and coarsely chopped

5 cloves garlic, smashed

5 star anise

4 boneless, skinless chicken breast halves

Kosher salt

¼ cup rice vinegar

¼ cup peanut oil

1 to 2 tablespoons chopped fresh cilantro (I toss in a small handful)

2 or 3 scallions, chopped, white and light green parts only (a small handful)

1 jalapeño, seeded and sliced

1 teaspoon grated fresh ginger

1 teaspoon grated garlic

1 teaspoon sriracha or similar hot pepper sauce

Juice of 1 lime

Splash of fish sauce

1 head red-leaf lettuce, leaves torn

Like a lot of folks, I much prefer chicken thighs to breasts for dishes with a lot of competing flavors; thighs are more forgiving and flavorful, in part because of their slightly higher fat content. But no worries! Not enough fat to warrant a call to the cardiologist. My family and I find this classic is just about perfect served over steaming hot rice or stuffed into tacos or pitas. And by the way, this also is an easygoing recipe if you find yourself cooking on set with Rachael Ray or Steve Harvey—or Rachael Ray *and* Steve Harvey . . . one of my oft-recurring dreams.

CHICKEN THIGHS ADOBO

SERVES 4

½ cup all-purpose flour

2 pounds bone-in, skin-on chicken thighs

Kosher salt and freshly ground black pepper

2 tablespoons dark sesame oil

1 yellow onion, thinly sliced (about 1 cup)

3 cloves garlic, minced

4-inch knob fresh ginger, peeled, smashed, and minced

¼ cup soy sauce

¼ cup pineapple vinegar (Pok Pok Som brand) or white wine vinegar (see Notes)

2 tablespoons light brown sugar

2 Turkish bay leaves (see Notes)

3½ to 4 cups hot cooked white rice

Spread the flour in a shallow dish. Lightly season the chicken with salt and pepper and dredge with flour to coat. Let rest for a few minutes to give the flour time to set on the chicken.

In a large pot with a tight-fitting lid, heat 1 tablespoon of the oil. Add the onions, garlic, and ginger and cook, stirring so that the garlic doesn't burn, until the onions start to soften, 3 to 4 minutes. Add the remaining 1 tablespoon oil and then the chicken thighs, skin side down. Cook the chicken without moving it for 3 to 4 minutes. Turn the chicken and brown on the other side. Add the soy sauce, vinegar, sugar, bay leaves, and ¼ cup water. Stir gently to mix, and season to taste with salt and pepper.

Cover the pot tightly and braise the chicken at a low simmer until an instant-read thermometer registers 180°F when inserted into the thickest part of a thigh, 1 hour to 1 hour and 15 minutes. Adjust the heat up or down to maintain the simmer and, if necessary, add a few tablespoons of water if the pot looks like it's drying out.

Divide the rice among shallow bowls. Top it with the chicken and the pan juices and onions.

———

Notes: If you can find it, keep a bottle of pineapple vinegar in your pantry (it's pretty easy to find online). It's great with this chicken and adds its own tropical essence to any number of dishes that will perk up with a splash of sassy vin.

While you can substitute ordinary bay leaves for the Turkish leaves here, try to find them. They are sold in many supermarkets, specialty markets, and online. Their flavor is slightly milder than other bays, and yet at the same time they add a complexity of flavors not ordinarily associated with bay leaves.

Who can resist crispy duck skin that gives way to supple, yielding, moist meat? I can't, which is why I suggest you make this "times two" because you're sure to want seconds. Or—gasp!—you can indulge in cold fried duck confit tomorrow.

FRIED DUCK CONFIT
WITH EUCALYPTUS HONEY AND MUSTARD GREENS

In a large mixing bowl, toss the salt with the thyme, cloves, coriander seeds, and bay leaf. Bury the duck legs in the salt mixture, adding more salt if needed to cover them completely. Set aside for about 3 hours at room temperature.

Preheat the oven to 325°F.

Lift the duck legs from the salt and wipe off the salt clinging to them. Transfer the legs to a deep, heavy baking dish and add the duck fat so that it covers them. Roast the duck legs for 4 to 5 hours, until very tender. Remove the dish from the oven and let it cool to lukewarm. Refrigerate the duck legs, still covered with the fat, for at least 4 hours or longer.

Stir together the honey, vinegar, and chile. Add the mint, cilantro, and a few red pepper flakes, if using. Set aside to give the chile time to infuse the sauce. Just before serving, warm the sauce in the microwave (or on top of the stove in a small saucepan). Do not cook it, but warm it enough so that it drizzles easily over the duck.

Lift the duck legs from the fat and wipe off the excess.

Put the buttermilk in a shallow bowl and the flour in another. Dip the duck legs first in the buttermilk and then in the flour. Repeat to coat them twice. Set them on a platter while the oil heats.

Pour the oil into a deep, heavy pot to a depth of 3 to 4 inches. Heat over medium-high heat until a deep-frying thermometer registers 360°F. Fry the duck legs for 2 to 3 minutes on each side, until nicely browned and crispy. Drain on paper towels.

Serve the duck and mustard greens together and pass the honey sauce on the side.

2 to 3 cups coarse salt

2 to 3 tablespoons dried thyme

1 tablespoon whole cloves

1 tablespoon coriander seeds

1 bay leaf

8 duck legs

2 cups duck fat, melted

½ cup eucalyptus honey, or your favorite type

¼ cup white wine vinegar

1 fresh serrano chile, seeded and sliced

Small handful fresh mint leaves (optional)

Small handful fresh cilantro leaves (optional)

Red pepper flakes (optional)

2 cups buttermilk

1½ cups all-purpose flour

Vegetable oil, for frying

Mustard Greens (page 201)

Spatchcock is one of my favorite words. Because obviously I'm a 12-year-old boy. But it's also one of my favorite butchering techniques, as it enables you to cook a whole bird, any bird, evenly on a grill or in a pan. Here it's part of a sweet and spicy Caribbean combo. (But for extra giggles, serve it with cockles.)

JERKED SPATCHCOCK
CHICKEN AND PLANTAINS

SERVES 4

One 2½- to 3-pound chicken

1 cup orange juice

2 tablespoons extra-virgin olive oil

2 cloves garlic, minced

2 teaspoons jerk spices

Peanut or canola oil, for frying

3 large black-skinned plantains

Kosher salt

2 or 3 scallions, sliced, white and light green parts only

2 tablespoons chopped fresh cilantro

Pepper vinegar, for serving (see Note)

Mango chutney, for serving

Spatchcock the chicken by removing the backbone and opening the chicken like a book so that it lies nearly flat. Slide out the breast cartilage.

In a shallow glass, ceramic, or other nonreactive bowl, stir together the orange juice, olive oil, garlic, and jerk spices. Flatten the chicken in the marinade so that it's covered as completely as possible. Cover and refrigerate the chicken for at least 1 hour and up to 12 hours or overnight.

Prepare a gas or charcoal grill so that the heating elements or coals are medium-hot.

Lift the chicken from the marinade and let any excess drip back into the pan. Lightly pat the chicken with paper towels to remove excess moisture and then lay the bird on the grill, skin side down. Grill the chicken for 25 to 30 minutes, turning it several times. It's done when the juices run clear or when an instant-read thermometer inserted into the thickest part of the thigh registers 170°F. Remove the chicken from the grill and let it rest, loosely covered with aluminum foil.

In a large skillet, heat about 1 inch of the peanut oil until hot. Cook the plantains in a single layer until browned, 3 to 4 minutes on each side, in batches if necessary to avoid overcrowding. Drain on paper towels and sprinkle lightly with salt while still hot.

With a heavy knife, cut the spatchcocked chicken into 8 or 10 pieces (you might want to cut the breasts in half if they are large). Transfer the chicken to a serving platter and garnish with scallions, cilantro, and fried plantains. Serve with the pepper vinegar and mango chutney on the side.

———

Note: Pepper vinegar is exactly that: vinegar flavored with peppers, or to be more accurate, chiles. Many people make their own, stuffing halved or coarsely chopped fresh chiles (any that you have on hand or that you especially like) into bottles or jars and then topping them with vinegar (usually cider vin). After 3 to 4 weeks, you have a pepper sauce to reckon with. Or you can buy pepper vin online, from fancy markets, and at some farmer's markets.

You didn't know you could make squab à l'orange, did you? Easy! You can always substitute chicken, but try to find squab, which is simply young pigeon. Farm-raised or wild, up to you. I don't recommend a New York City pigeon (although I've always believed that there's got to be a way to sustainably and safely harness their numbers as a food source). Seriously, squab is one of my favorites: meaty and gamy, with a flavor that's more intense than duck, which explains why I chose squab for this classic. And its size—which can't be much more than a pound before it's designated pigeon—makes it perfect for a hungry person. So the next time you're camped on a park bench, consider, as I do, that the ever-present pigeons might taste like pizza, since they snack on discarded crusts all day long.

SQUAB WITH ORANGES
AND ALMONDS

In a large, deep pot with a tight-fitting lid, heat the duck fat over high heat. When hot, reduce the heat to medium-high, add the celery, carrots, and onion, and cook, stirring, until the onions are tender and fragrant, 4 to 5 minutes. Add the squab and thyme and cook until the squab are lightly browned on both sides, 2 to 3 minutes, turning the squab once during browning.

Season to taste with salt and pepper. Add the stock, port, and grated orange zest and stir gently to mix. Cover and cook until the squab are cooked through, about 20 minutes.

Lift the squab from the pot and set aside to rest on a plate. Strain the liquid through a fine-mesh sieve into a saucepan. Bring to a boil over medium-high heat, immediately reduce the heat to medium, and simmer until the liquid reduces by half, 8 to 10 minutes. Stir in the orange juice and season to taste with salt and pepper. Cook over medium heat until the sauce is smooth and nearly as thick as heavy cream, 5 to 10 minutes.

Pour the warm sauce into shallow bowls and top with a squab. Garnish with the slivered orange zest, almonds, and orange segments and orange blossoms or leaves, if using.

Note: To toast the slivered almonds, spread the nuts in a small, dry skillet and toast them over medium heat for a minute or so, gently shaking the pan until they turn a shade darker and are aromatic.

SERVES 4

2 tablespoons duck fat or unsalted butter

2 stalks celery, chopped

2 carrots, chopped

1 yellow onion, chopped (about 1 cup)

4 squab, each about 1 pound, wing tips removed

3 sprigs fresh thyme

Kosher salt and freshly ground black pepper

1 quart veal or chicken stock, preferably homemade

¼ cup port wine

Zest and juice of 3 navel oranges; grate the zest of 1 orange and sliver the zest of the other 2 for garnish

½ cup slivered almonds, toasted (see Note)

2 oranges, peeled and divided into segments (optional)

4 sprigs orange blossoms or leaves, for garnish (optional)

I'd tag this one of my most straightforward dishes, and one of the smartest. I minimize the typical appeal of duck with sweet ingredients by relying on the natural sweetness of carrots that have simmered in gentle chamomile tea before being paired with the duck. The underplaying of sweetness means you can really take in the gaminess of the bird. I like using tea bags for subtle flavor, and perhaps the chamomile will open the door for using other flavors of tea to enhance different vegetables and meats.

DUCK BREASTS WITH
CARROTS AND CHAMOMILE

SERVES 4

2 whole duck breasts

1 to 2 teaspoons French 4-spice blend (your favorite brand) (see Note)

1 pound baby carrots, halved or quartered if large

2 chamomile tea bags

2 tablespoons unsalted butter, sliced

1 teaspoon honey

Kosher salt

2 cups veal or chicken stock, preferably homemade

1 tablespoon cornstarch

2 mandarin oranges, peeled and chopped

1 bunch fresh flat-leaf parsley, thick stems discarded and leaves chopped, for garnish

Chamomile or coriander flowers, for garnish (optional)

Preheat the oven to 350°F.

Score the duck breasts in several places. This will allow the duck fat to escape during cooking. Season lightly with the spice blend.

Heat a large, oven-safe skillet over medium-high heat. When hot, sear the duck breasts, skin side down, until the skin is crispy and golden brown and the fat renders, 4 to 5 minutes. Lift the duck breasts from the pan and drain off the fat. (Reserve the fat for another use.) Return the duck breasts to the pan, skin side up.

Transfer the skillet to the oven and roast the duck breasts for 8 to 10 minutes, until cooked through. Lift the duck breasts from the skillet and set them aside to rest.

Meanwhile, put the carrots in a large saucepan and add enough cold water to cover by about ½ inch. Add the tea bags, butter, and honey and season lightly with salt. Bring to a boil over medium-high heat and cook until the water evaporates and the carrots are tender and glazed, 10 to 12 minutes.

Mix 1 tablespoon of the stock with the cornstarch to make a slurry, stirring well until smooth and lump-free.

In a saucepan, heat the remaining stock over medium heat until warm. Add the slurry to the warm stock and whisk until thick and bubbling hot. Whisk in a little duck fat, if desired. Stir in the chopped mandarin oranges.

Slice the duck meat from the breasts. Arrange the sliced duck on plates and spoon some sauce over the meat. Pile the carrots next to the duck and serve garnished with chopped parsley and chamomile or coriander flowers, if desired.

———

Note: While you can make your own spice blend, you can also buy French 4-spice blend online or in shops that sell gourmet spice blends. It's used throughout France and also in the Middle East and always contains ground pepper (white or black), cloves, nutmeg, and ginger. Some folks add a few more spices, too, such as cinnamon or allspice. That would then make it a 5- or 6-spice blend, respectively.

I live in California now, and plenty of rabbits make their home in the coastal chaparral biome where I live and run. I say this in case you see me running unusually fast on a trail, chasing a brown blur. Rabbit needs a slow cook, and the flavors in this interpreted French classic lean a little toward Italy when I introduce currants and chocolate to the mix. Rascally rabbit . . .

RABBIT AU VIN

Season the rabbit with salt and pepper and put in a large plastic bag with a zip-top closure. Pour the wine into the bag and seal. Let sit at room temperature for about 15 minutes, or while you cook the bacon and vegetables.

In a large deep skillet, cook the bacon over medium heat until browned but not crisp. With a slotted spoon, lift the bacon from the skillet and drain on paper towels. Pour out all but about 1 tablespoon of the bacon fat.

Add the onions, mushrooms, and garlic to the skillet and cook, stirring, until the vegetables caramelize, about 10 minutes. Stir in the 2 tea-spoons butter and the flour and cook, stirring, to coat the veggies with the flour and give the butter time to melt.

Lift the rabbit from the plastic bag and add to the skillet. Reserve the wine. Raise the heat to medium-high and cook the rabbit for 2 to 4 minutes on each side, turning until evenly browned. Add the reserved wine and bring to a simmer, scraping up the browned bits from the bottom of the pan with a wooden spoon.

Add the bacon, stock, and thyme and season to taste with salt and pepper. Bring to a boil over medium-high heat. Lower the heat to medium, cover the skillet, and simmer until the rabbit is cooked through, about 1 hour.

Remove the lid and stir in the remaining 1 tablespoon butter, the chocolate, parsley, and currants. Cook for a few more minutes, stirring, until the butter is incorporated and the chocolate pretty much melted and combined.

To serve, discard the thyme and ladle the stew into shallow bowls, being sure to include a piece of the rabbit in each bowl.

SERVES 4

One 3-pound rabbit, cut into 4 pieces

Kosher salt and freshly ground black pepper

2 cups red wine

1 cup diced bacon (6 to 8 slices)

1 yellow onion, cut into small dice

12 white button mushrooms, quartered

2 cloves garlic, minced

1 tablespoon plus 2 teaspoons unsalted butter

2 teaspoons all-purpose flour

2 cups chicken stock, preferably homemade

6 sprigs fresh thyme

1½ ounces unsweetened chocolate, finely chopped

½ cup chopped fresh flat-leaf parsley

1 to 2 tablespoons dried currants (I toss in a small handful)

Adapted from The Crack Shack in San Diego, where we serve chicken and eggs all day long. The buttermilk brine provides just enough sourness, and the spice blend affords some pretty assertive heat. What you're going for in the texture department is crispy, golden chicken with lots of crevices and fissures in the fried coating. Giving the chicken a good shake once it's been coated in the spiced flour should do the trick. For a quick side sauce, mix a little honey with vinegar and a minced jalapeño. I also recommend serving this with a mandatory treadmill session.

CRACK SHACK FRIED
CHICKEN, NASHVILLE-STYLE

Put the chicken in a glass, ceramic, or other nonreactive dish. Pour the pickle juice over the chicken and turn to coat. Cover and refrigerate for about 1 hour, turning several times to ensure all the chicken pieces are flavored with the pickle juice.

Meanwhile, in another dish, whisk together the buttermilk and hot sauce. Season with salt and pepper.

Lift the chicken from the pickle juice and submerge it in the buttermilk marinade. Turn the chicken to coat, cover, and refrigerate for at least 6 hours and up to 12 hours or overnight.

To make the spice mix, in a mixing bowl, stir together the paprika, cayenne, brown sugar, garlic powder, onion powder, ginger, and salt.

Lift the chicken from the marinade and lay it on a baking sheet. Sprinkle the spice mix over the chicken and let sit for about 10 minutes to give the spice mix time to flavor the chicken.

Meanwhile, spread the flour and karaage mix in a large shallow bowl or dish and stir to mix. Dip the chicken in the flour to coat both sides. Shake the chicken to knock off some of the flour and distribute the flour that stays on the bird. Refrigerate the coated chicken on the baking sheet for 30 minutes before frying.

Pour oil into a deep, heavy pot to reach a depth of 3 to 4 inches. Heat over medium-high heat until a deep-frying thermometer reaches 350°F.

When the oil reaches the desired temperature, use tongs to put the chicken in the oil. Do not crowd the pan; you might have to fry the chicken in batches. Turn the chicken several times to brown it on all sides. Once it's lightly browned, let it cook without turning for 18 to 20 minutes. When it's done, an instant-read thermometer will register about 165°F when inserted into a meaty part of the chicken. (Take a piece of chicken out of the fryer before you check the temp! The oil is very hot.)

Lift the chicken from the pot and set on a wire rack sitting over a baking sheet to drain. If frying in batches, let the oil regain its temperature before cooking the next batch.

Let the chicken cool for about 10 minutes before serving.

———

Note: Karaage is a style of fried chicken (and other foods) developed in Japan. First, the food is flavored with ginger, garlic, and soy sauce, and then it's coated with potato starch or flour. If you can't find a commercial karaage mix, double the amount of all-purpose flour and season it generously with garlic powder, ground ginger, salt, and pepper.

SERVES 4

3 pounds whole chicken thighs, legs and thighs separated

¾ cup pickle juice (from a jar of your favorite pickles)

½ cup buttermilk

¼ cup Frank's RedHot sauce

Kosher salt and freshly ground black pepper

SPICE MIX

¼ cup plus 2 teaspoons sweet paprika

2 tablespoons cayenne pepper

2 tablespoons light brown sugar

2 tablespoons garlic powder

2 tablespoons onion powder

1 tablespoon ground ginger

1 teaspoon kosher salt

TO FRY

About 2 cups all-purpose flour

About 2 cups karaage seasoning mix (see Note)

Canola, vegetable, or peanut oil, for frying

The key to a good broth for ramen is using enough meat and bones and then cooking it long enough. Come to think of it, that's pretty much the key to any stock. For the stock in this recipe, I rely on charcuterie (cold cuts and sausages— even hot dogs). These are aged, heavily salted meats that contain lots of monosodium glutamate (MSG) for strong flavor. And, when you come right down to it, there always seems to be a nub of salami in my refrigerator.

As for the noodles, you can make your own if you're super ambitious, or just use Italian pasta. Of course, if you're able to get your hands on soba noodles, use them. It's leftover ramen, not rocket science.

RAMEN WITH LEFTOVERS

In a large pot, mix together the chicken carcass, ham, salami, hot dogs, two-thirds of the scallions, the carrots, garlic, ginger, kombu, and bonito flakes. Add the stock and soy sauce and bring to a boil over high heat. Skim any foam that rises to the surface and reduce the heat to medium. Simmer, uncovered, for 3 to 4 hours, adding more stock or water if necessary to keep the solids covered with liquid and adjusting the heat up or down to maintain a low simmer.

Remove the stock from the heat and strain through a colander. Discard the solids, reserving the hot dogs if they look good.

Divide the pasta, chicken, nori, and hot dogs, if using, among shallow bowls. Ladle the hot broth over them.

Garnish each serving with chili oil, sesame oil, togarashi, and the remaining scallions. Peel and halve the eggs and top each serving with an egg half.

———

Note: Also called dashima or konbu, kombu is edible kelp popular throughout Asia and growing in popularity here. Togarashi is a spicy Japanese seasoning that always includes red pepper flakes. Both kombu and togarashi are available in Asian markets and online.

SERVES 4

1 chicken carcass, coarsely chopped and broken apart

1 cup chopped ham

1 cup diced salami

2 hot dogs or any uncooked sausages

3 bunches scallions, chopped, white and light green parts only

2 carrots, diced

Cloves from 1 head garlic, smashed

1-inch knob fresh ginger, peeled and smashed

1 piece kombu (see Note)

¼ cup bonito flakes

2 quarts chicken stock, plus more if needed, preferably homemade

1 tablespoon soy sauce

2 cups cooked noodles, such as soba noodles, linguine, or thin spaghetti (about 4 ounces uncooked)

1 cup chopped cooked chicken or turkey

2 nori sheets, cut into quarters

Chili oil, for garnish

Dark sesame oil, for garnish

Togarashi, for garnish (see Note)

2 large soft-boiled eggs

I could have named this Christmas Goose Pastilla, as the pastry here resembles the one that comes out of North Africa, but *strudel* sounds better, right? Especially around Christmastime, although you don't have to make this only during the holidays. While it's great any time of year, the question remains: Who would make goose strudel (other than me)? You! So, meet an amazing ingredient with an incredible savoriness. Plus, rendered goose fat takes this—or any dish—to the next level.

CHRISTMAS GOOSE
STRUDEL

In a large sauté pan, heat the oil over medium-high heat. When hot, add the onion and garlic and cook, stirring, until the onion begins to soften, about 2 minutes. Add the meat and flour and cook, stirring, for another 1 to 2 minutes.

Add the spice mix, stir, and then add the raisins and dates. Season with the cinnamon and salt to taste and stir well to mix all the ingredients. Add the chicken stock and almonds, if using. The mixture will look like a pie filling—which it is.

Let the filling cool to lukewarm, and then transfer to a bowl and refrigerate for at least 1 hour and up to 12 hours or overnight.

Preheat the oven to 350°F.

Lay 1 sheet of phyllo on a work surface and brush with melted butter. Top with another sheet, brush with melted butter, and continue until all 5 sheets are stacked and brushed.

Spread the goose filling along one side of the phyllo and roll it into a log (like a burrito). Transfer to a baking sheet and brush with more butter.

Bake for about 30 minutes, or until the phyllo is golden brown and the filling is bubbling hot. (Alternatively, spread the filling in a pie plate, top it with the phyllo, and bake.)

Sprinkle with the crushed almonds and sugar, slice, and serve.

———

Note: There are other names for the spice mix I like to use with the goose: tagine spices, natural Moroccan spice blend, and *ras el hanout*. You can buy these blends online and at stores that sell North African ingredients. The flavor profile includes warm, heady spices such as cumin, ginger, cinnamon, allspice, and cloves. There might be cayenne, too, for a little bite.

SERVES 4

1 tablespoon vegetable oil

½ yellow onion, chopped (about ½ cup)

2 cloves garlic, chopped

2 cups chopped leftover cooked goose, duck, or turkey

A few pinches of all-purpose flour

2 to 3 teaspoons Moroccan spice mix (see Note)

3 tablespoons golden or dark raisins (I usually opt for golden)

2 or 3 dates, chopped, or 1 tablespoon candied ginger

About ½ teaspoon ground cinnamon

Kosher salt

½ cup chicken stock, preferably homemade

2 tablespoons chopped or sliced almonds (optional)

5 sheets packaged frozen phyllo dough

4 tablespoons (½ stick) unsalted butter, melted

1 to 2 tablespoons crushed almonds

1 tablespoon raw sugar

Okay. I agree. This is a laborious take on traditional Thanksgiving flavors, but if you're the kind of cook who likes to impress, you probably enjoy both the process and the craft. And the thought of how many "likes" you'll get for the photo is exhilarating. Go for it!

BONELESS TURDUCKEN
WITH MASHED RUTABAGAS AND CRANBERRY SAUCE

SERVES 6 TO 8

One 4- to 5-pound boneless, skinless turkey breast

Kosher salt and freshly ground black pepper

One 1-pound boneless, skinless duck breast

One 12-ounce boneless, skinless chicken breast

About 7 cups chicken stock, plus more if needed, preferably homemade

3 tablespoons unsalted butter

2 cloves garlic, finely chopped

2 or 3 fresh sage leaves, chopped

1 sprig fresh rosemary, leaves chopped

Mashed Rutabagas (page 212)

Canned jellied cranberry sauce, for serving (canned is the best!)

Spread the turkey breast on a work surface so that it's as open as possible. Lay a sheet of plastic wrap over it and, using a meat mallet or the bottom of a small heavy skillet, gently pound the turkey until it's as uniformly thin as possible. Remove the plastic wrap and season the turkey with salt and pepper. Repeat with the duck breast and then with the chicken breast.

Lay the duck breast on top of the turkey breast. Lay the chicken breast on top of the duck breast. Beginning at a long end, roll the 3 breasts into a log. Tie the log closed by winding kitchen twine along its length, as you would a roast. Tie the turducken as firmly and tightly as you can.

In a large pot, bring the chicken stock to a boil, reduce the heat and put the roast in the simmering liquid. Add more stock or water to the pot if it does not just cover the roast. Poach for 45 minutes to 1 hour or until an instant-read thermometer inserted into a thick part of the roast registers 160°F. When done, lift the roast from the poaching liquid, keeping it tied with twine. Pat it dry with paper towels.

In a large skillet, melt the butter over medium heat. Add the garlic, sage, and rosemary. Raise the heat a little, add the turducken log, and sear until it's browned on all sides, basting with the buttery pan sauce during searing.

Remove the turducken from the heat and remove the twine. Slice the turducken and serve it with rutabagas alongside. Pass the cranberry sauce on the side.

Goulash is the cilantro of the casserole world—either you love it or you hate it. I love it, needless to say. Topping each serving with a fried egg creates a rich, luscious sauce when the yolks break, which enhances the dish's wintry vibe. Ladle the goulash over homemade spaetzle and this is ready for a menu somewhere in Brooklyn or San Francisco. Or in your own kitchen. I like to make the goulash with duck legs, but it would be very good with chicken legs.

DUCK GOULASH AND
SPAETZLE WITH FRIED DUCK EGGS

To make the duck, lightly season the duck legs with salt and pepper. Spread the flour on a plate and dredge the duck legs with the flour until lightly coated.

In a large deep skillet or large pot, heat the olive oil over medium-high heat. When hot, brown the duck legs on all sides, using tongs to turn them. Remove the duck legs and set aside.

Reduce the heat to low, add the butter, and, when it melts, add the garlic, onions, caraway seeds, and paprika. Cook, stirring, until the mixture is aromatic and the onions are translucent, about 3 minutes. Stir in the tomato paste and, when thoroughly incorporated, slowly add the stock and wine, stirring constantly.

Return the duck legs to the pan, being sure to include any accumulated juices. Add the tomatoes, cover the pan, and cook until the duck meat is tender, 50 to 60 minutes. Lift the duck legs from the pan and pull or slice the meat from the legs, discarding the bones. Return the meat to the pan and stir to mix. Cover to keep warm (you may have to reheat the goulash before serving).

To make the spaetzle, bring a stockpot filled about halfway with water to a boil.

In a large bowl, stir together the flour, eggs, milk, and 1 teaspoon of salt until smooth. The dough will be tacky.

Transfer the dough to a spaetzle maker; or coat a wide mesh colander with flavorless cooking spray and transfer the dough to that. Set the spaetzle maker or colander over the boiling water and use a wooden spoon to press on the dough so that small pieces drop into the boiling water.

Cook until the spaetzle are tender and float to the surface, about 2 minutes. Remove with a slotted spoon to drain, and put in a serving bowl. Add the butter, season lightly with salt, and toss to coat. Sprinkle the hot spaetzle with chopped parsley and toss to mix.

To make the garnish, heat the butter in a large nonstick skillet over medium-high heat. Crack the eggs into the pan and cook until the whites are just set but not browned or bubbly. Remove the pan from the heat. Alternatively, crack the eggs and carefully separate the yolks

SERVES 4

DUCK

4 duck or chicken legs

Kosher salt and freshly ground black pepper

2 tablespoons all-purpose flour

2 tablespoons extra-virgin olive oil

1 tablespoon unsalted butter

4 cloves garlic, minced

2 red onions, diced

1 tablespoon caraway seeds, toasted (see Note)

1½ teaspoons hot paprika

1½ teaspoons tomato paste

3 cups duck or chicken stock, preferably homemade

½ cup red wine

1 cup drained and chopped canned tomatoes

SPAETZLE

2 cups all-purpose flour

4 large eggs, lightly beaten

⅓ cup whole milk

Kosher salt

1 tablespoon unsalted butter

1 small bunch fresh flat-leaf parsley, chopped, for garnish

GARNISH

1 tablespoon unsalted butter

4 duck eggs or large chicken eggs

2 tablespoons balsamic vinegar

Kosher salt and freshly ground black pepper

from the whites. Reserve the whites for another use. Garnish the goulash with the raw yolks rather than fried eggs.

Divide the spaetzle among shallow bowls. Ladle the goulash over it, being sure to top each serving with a duck leg. Set an egg on top of each serving and drizzle with vinegar. Season lightly with salt and pepper, and serve.

Note: To toast the caraway seeds, spread them in a single layer in a small frying pan and toast over medium heat for 45 to 60 seconds. Shake the pan to promote even toasting. When the seeds darken a shade and are aromatic, slide them onto a plate to cool.

I think of this roast chicken with all its drippings and a splash of spicy, sweet vinegar as more than crave-worthy: It's heavenly. Serve it as the main attraction, or pick the bird apart for tacos or sandwiches or salads.

ROAST CHICKEN
WITH PINEAPPLE VINEGAR AND CHILE

SERVES 4

One 4-pound chicken

¼ cup soy sauce

¼ cup pineapple juice

¼ cup pineapple vinegar (Pok Pok Som brand)

1 tablespoon minced peeled fresh ginger

1 teaspoon dark sesame oil

3 cloves garlic, minced

2 cups chopped scallions

1 fresh Fresno chile, seeded and chopped

Kosher salt and freshly ground black pepper

1 cup (2 sticks) unsalted butter, at room temperature

1 bunch fresh cilantro, chopped

Rinse the chicken and pat it dry. Tie the legs together with kitchen twine and tuck the wing tips under the body of the chicken.

In a glass, ceramic, or rigid plastic dish large enough to hold the chicken, mix together the soy sauce, pineapple juice, pineapple vinegar, ginger, sesame oil, and garlic. Add 1 cup of the chopped scallions and the chile. Season lightly with salt and pepper. Submerge the chicken in the marinade, turning to coat. Cover the dish and refrigerate the chicken in its marinade for at least 1 hour and up to 12 hours or overnight, turning the chicken several times to ensure even coating.

In another bowl, mix the butter with the remaining 1 cup scallions and the cilantro. Season to taste with salt and pepper.

Preheat the oven to 400°F.

Lift the chicken from the marinade and pat it dry with paper towels. Put the chicken in a roasting pan. Using your fingers, loosen the skin covering the breast meat. Do not detach or remove it. Slide the butter under the skin and over the meat, distributing it as evenly as you can.

Roast the chicken for 45 to 50 minutes, until cooked through and an instant-read thermometer registers 165°F when inserted in the breast meat. The juices will run clear, too, when the meat is cut into. Let the chicken rest for 5 to 10 minutes before carving and serving.

BEEF, PORK, LAMB, AND GOAT

We Americans love meat. We could eat it at every meal, regardless of where we are in the country. And once you push beyond grilled steak and pork chops, options for cooking meat seem endless, particularly when we look to the horizon and explore how other cultures treat pork, lamb, and beef. And goat. Don't forget goat!

A quick perusal of this chapter demonstrates how much I like slow-cooked dishes, which result in perfectly cooked, moist, tender meat.

With these recipes, I encourage readers to consider the so-called lesser cuts of meat, like oxtail and ham hocks. Full of amazing flavor but currently out of favor with some of us. Let's change that, people! This is home cooking at its best.

I've always liked the idea of cooking in milk. It makes a sauce that is deliciously custard-like and just a little broken—very similar to the sausage gravy so often found in Southern cooking. Stands to reason that biscuits would be a natural accompaniment.

MILK-BRAISED PORK
SHOULDER WITH BUTTERMILK BISCUITS AND GRAVY

SERVES 8 TO 10

1 tablespoon fennel seeds

2 teaspoons garlic powder

One 6- to 8-pound bone-in pork neck or shoulder

Kosher salt and freshly ground black pepper

2 tablespoons vegetable oil

2 cups whole milk, or more as necessary

1 tablespoon whole cloves

2 or 3 fresh sage leaves

1 bay leaf

About ¼ cup condensed milk

Buttermilk Biscuits (page 213)

Gently rub the fennel seeds and garlic powder into the meat. Season lightly with salt and pepper.

In a deep pot with a lid, heat the oil over medium-high heat. When hot, sear the pork neck on all sides until golden brown. Add the whole milk. It should nearly cover the meat; if not, add a little more. Bring the milk to a simmer, scraping up any bits of meat sticking to the bottom of the pan.

Add the cloves, sage, and bay leaf to the pot, cover, and braise on top of the stove over medium-low heat until the pork is cooked through and registers 155°F on an instant-read thermometer, 2 to 3 hours. Lift the pork from the milk and set on a platter.

Strain the milk to remove the cloves, sage, and bay leaves. Return the milk to the pot and add the pork. Cook until the milk is slightly thickened and reduced, about 10 minutes. Add the condensed milk to thicken and sweeten the salty piggy milk. Taste and season with salt and pepper, if needed.

Slice the pork and serve alongside hot buttermilk biscuits smothered in the milky gravy.

Lemongrass is such a bear to handle and chop that I turn to liquid nitrogen. It makes it easy to turn those sinewy stalks of lemongrass into powder so that you can use a good amount to intensify the flavor of this beef stew. Plus, I'm contractually obligated to feature three recipes in this book that employ liquid nitrogen. If you don't want to use it, simply chop the lemongrass stalks with a heavy knife.

SHORT RIBS WITH
LEMONGRASS

If using the liquid nitrogen, carefully pour it into a stainless steel bowl. Drop the lemongrass into the liquid nitrogen and smash the stalks into pieces with a spoon. Strain the liquid nitrogen through a sieve. You should have 3 to 4 tablespoons smashed lemongrass.

If not using liquid nitrogen, use a heavy, sharp knife to chop the lemongrass. You should have about ¼ cup chopped lemongrass.

In a large, deep pot with a tight-fitting lid, heat the oil over high heat until shimmering hot. Reduce the heat to medium-high and add the beef short ribs to the pan, turning until browned on all sides. Season with salt and pepper. Lift the short ribs from the pot and set aside.

Add the onions and garlic and cook, stirring, until the onions are translucent, about 2 minutes, taking care that the garlic does not burn. Add the lemongrass, tomato paste, ginger, star anise, and whole Thai chile and cook, stirring, until aromatic, about 5 minutes.

Add the short ribs and any accumulated juices to the pot, along with 1 cup of the daikon and the carrots. Pour in the beef stock and fish sauce.

Cover the pot with the lid and braise over medium-low heat until a big chunk of meat registers at least 130°F on an instant-read thermometer or until it's done to your liking, 1 to 1½ hours, watching the heat and adjusting up or down to maintain a gentle simmer. When done, remove the star anise and whole chile.

Ladle the stew into bowls, and serve garnished with the remaining ¼ cup daikon and the basil.

SERVES 4

1 quart liquid nitrogen (optional)

7 or 8 stalks lemongrass, outer layers removed and tops and bottoms trimmed

3 tablespoons grapeseed oil

3 to 4 pounds boneless beef short ribs

Kosher salt and freshly ground black pepper

1 yellow onion, finely diced (1 scant cup)

2 cloves garlic, minced

3 tablespoons tomato paste

1-inch knob fresh ginger, peeled and smashed (use the broad side of a large knife)

2 star anise

1 fresh Thai chile

1 large daikon radish, diced (about 1¼ cups)

3 carrots, diced (about 1½ cups)

1½ quarts beef stock, preferably homemade

2 tablespoons fish sauce

¼ cup loosely packed chopped fresh Thai basil (3 or 4 sprigs)

A hamburger stuffed with warm melted cheese is one of the few foods that fall into the camps of both modernist molecular cuisine and stoner food. It's easy to imagine a few kids sitting on the hood of a car in a convenience store parking lot, concocting this bad boy. Truth is, it was created in a Minneapolis restaurant. I like to crown it with caramelized onions and some easy-to-make bread-and-butter pickles. Serve it on a toasted brioche bun, with ketchup and mustard if you like. And no one will refuse fries on the plate.

JUICY LUCY

SERVES 4

2 cucumbers, cut crosswise into ⅛-inch-thick rounds

Kosher salt

3 cups apple cider vinegar

½ cup sugar

1 teaspoon yellow mustard seeds

1 teaspoon ground turmeric

1½ tablespoons unsalted butter

1 yellow onion, thinly sliced (about 1 cup)

1 pound ground brisket

8 ounces ground chuck

8 ounces ground short rib (see Notes)

½ cup dry-aged fat (see Notes)

4 slices American cheese

Freshly ground black pepper

4 brioche buns, lightly toasted

Ketchup and mustard, for serving (optional)

Put the cucumbers in a glass or ceramic bowl and season generously with salt. Let the cucumbers sit for at least 30 minutes, until the salt draws the moisture from the cukes. Rinse well and transfer the cucumbers to another large glass or ceramic bowl.

Meanwhile, in a large nonreactive saucepan, combine the vinegar with the sugar, mustard seeds, and turmeric. Bring to a boil over medium-high heat and cook, stirring occasionally, until the sugar dissolves.

Pour 1 cup of the hot pickling liquid over the cucumbers and set aside to steep. Reserve the remaining pickling liquid for another time. It will keep in the refrigerator for 2 weeks, stored in a lidded glass container.

In a large skillet, melt the butter over medium heat. Add the onions and toss to coat with the butter. Cover and slowly cook, stirring occasionally, until softened, 5 to 6 minutes. Increase the heat to medium-high and brown the onions, stirring constantly, for 6 to 8 minutes longer. When caramelized, season the onions with salt and set aside.

Prepare a charcoal or gas grill for indirect, medium-high heat, or heat a grill pan over high heat.

In a large bowl, use your hands to mix together the ground brisket, ground chuck, ground short ribs, and fat until thoroughly incorporated. Shape into eight 1-inch-thick patties.

Cut 1 slice of American cheese into 4 squares and stack them on top of each other. Put the cheese stack between 2 patties and press the edges of the patties to seal them; don't leave any cracks. This is very important because you do not want the cheese to ooze out during cooking. Repeat with the remaining patties and cheese so you have 4 Juicy Lucys.

Season the patties on both sides with salt and pepper. Grill the patties over direct heat for 2 to 3 minutes on each side. Move the patties over indirect heat on the grill and cook for 2 to 3 minutes more. If using a grill pan, reduce the heat slightly for the final 2 to 3 minutes of cooking.

Serve the patties on brioche buns topped with the onions and pickles. Serve with ketchup and mustard, if desired.

———

Notes: If your butcher does not carry ground short rib meat, make up the difference with equal amounts of chuck and brisket.

Aged fat is the fat found on aged beef. You may have to special-order it from the butcher. If you can't find it, use any beef fat. (If you can't find it or if you just can't do it, leave it out. I won't tell . . . although the burger is best when the fat is included.)

Truth is, a few extra-large rib eye chops found their way into the kitchen during the photo shoot for this book. So we cooked them! With chops as big as these, think of this as a special-occasion dish when you want to celebrate in style. The potatoes are easy to make and show up on the Blais family table meal after meal. For authenticity, cook the spuds in seawater, but if you don't live on the beach, add sea salt to the cooking water instead.

RIB EYE CHOPS WITH
SEAWATER POTATOES

Put the potatoes and salt in a large pot and add enough cold water to cover the potatoes by about 2 inches. Bring to a boil over high heat. Lower the heat a little and simmer briskly until the potatoes can easily be pierced with a knife, about 15 minutes. You may need to add more water to the pot to fully cook the larger potatoes.

Meanwhile, liberally season the steaks with salt and pepper.

Heat a large frying pan over high heat and, when hot, pour the canola oil into it and let it heat until it just begins to smoke. Sear the steaks for about 4 minutes on each side for medium-rare.

Before removing the steaks from the pan, add the butter, thyme, and garlic. Baste both sides of the steaks with the melted butter sauce several times.

Remove the steaks and let them rest on a cutting board for about 2 minutes before serving.

SERVES 6 TO 8

3 pounds baby white potatoes

4 cups sea or kosher salt

6 to 8 bone-in rib eye steaks, each weighing 12 to 14 ounces

Sea salt and freshly ground black pepper

About 1 tablespoon canola oil

4 tablespoons (½ stick) unsalted butter

6 to 8 sprigs fresh thyme

6 to 8 cloves garlic, crushed

I grew a beard last winter so I'd be manly enough for this pot roast. It's a wintry treat with super tender short ribs that fall off their bones, served with a celery root puree that makes a rather posh mash. I'm a big fan of those pickled walnuts that come in a jar, and when they're part of the mix, the pot roast gains a certain maturity so rarely found in my food!

SHORT RIB POT ROAST
WITH CELERY ROOT PUREE AND PICKLED WALNUTS

SERVES 4 TO 6

One 750 ml bottle red wine, such as Zinfandel

2 carrots, peeled and coarsely chopped

1 yellow onion, coarsely chopped

1 bay leaf

Kosher salt and freshly ground black pepper

5 pounds beef short ribs

2 cups all-purpose flour

2 tablespoons vegetable oil

Celery Root Puree (page 211)

Pickled walnuts (from a jar), for garnish

In a glass, ceramic, or other nonreactive dish, mix together the wine, carrots, onions, and bay leaf. Season lightly with salt and pepper. Put the short ribs in the marinade, making sure they are covered with the liquid, cover, and refrigerate for at least 2 hours and up to 12 hours or overnight.

Spread the flour on a large plate and season it with salt and pepper.

Lift the short ribs from the marinade and let the excess drip back into the bowl. Strain and reserve the marinade. Use paper towels to blot the ribs dry. Dredge the ribs in the flour, coating both sides.

In a large skillet, heat the oil until hot over medium-high heat. Sear the short ribs until browned, 1 to 2 minutes on each side; do this in batches, taking care not to overcrowd the skillet.

In a large pot or Dutch oven, heat the reserved marinade until boiling. Add the short ribs to the pot and reduce the heat so that the liquid is barely simmering. Cover the pot and braise the short ribs until the meat practically falls off the bones, 3 to 4 hours.

Serve the short ribs with the Celery Root Puree and some pickled walnuts.

My Favorite Cooking Method

When I was studying at the CIA, my classmates nicknamed me Ritchie Braise. That's how much I love to cook foods slow and easy. And who doesn't like the iconic image of a big, steaming pot of delicious food being lifted from the oven?

While braising's first cousin is stewing, they're not identical. The differences lie with the amount of liquid and the size of the food. I braise an entire chuck roast, brisket, pork shoulder, and oversize carrots in only enough liquid to happily slosh around in the bottom of the pot. Stews are made with chunky, bite-size pieces of food that cook in more liquid, usually enough to cover the food.

Braised meats and other foods are tender and full flavored and you may not even need a knife to cut them. But if you ask me, that's not the best part of braises. The best part is the pan sauce that mingles with the vegetables and meat to impart so much goodness and comfort that you'll wonder why you don't braise more often. Like maybe every day!

Because I like to braise, I like to cook foods by sous vide, which roughly translates from the French as "under vacuum" cooking. For most sous vide, food is enclosed in a plastic bag. It's not zipped shut but is tightly sealed with a vacuum sealer (like a FoodSaver). The impervious plastic bag is then cooked for a long period of time in a hot water bath that maintains a constant but relatively low temperature. For this you need a sous vide cooker, either a large pot especially made for sous vide or an immersion water circulator that clips onto any ole pot and circulates the water during cooking to keep it at a set temperature. (Believe me, the sous vide pots are far more costly than the immersion circulators. Your choice depends on how often you plan to sous vide.)

Oven braising is still long and slow cooking. Don't let that put you off. I braise both on top of the stove and in the oven with equally good results. In fact, if you want to use the oven and my recipe calls for simmering the braise on top of the stove, go right ahead and put the covered pot in a 325°F oven for several hours. Use my stovetop time frame and your common sense to determine when it's done. And of course this works vice versa.

So go for it! Braised meats, poultry, and vegetables like carrots, leeks, potatoes, celeriac, and onions are some of life's simplest and tastiest pleasures. And guess what? It's easy. Once everything is in the pot, the braise cooks itself.

I don't want to preach, but we should all work for diversity in our diets, so how about goat? It's a heady, gamy meat that you just might fall in love with. Many have. Still, if it's hard to find, mutton works. Actually, any braised meat does. I season this with Jamaican curry powder, an addictive spice blend that should be part of your arsenal. I use it often in soups and on roasted vegetables. It's a little sweeter than it is spicy and is a great gateway spice to fuel future seasoning habits.

CURRIED GOAT POT PIE

Season the goat pieces with the curry powder and salt, tossing to mix well.

In a heavy pot with a tight-fitting lid, heat the oil over medium-high heat. When hot, sear the goat pieces until golden brown on all sides; you may have to do this in batches, as you don't want to crowd the pot.

When all the meat is nicely browned, return it to the pot (if you seared it in batches) and add the onions, carrots, and celery. Stir to mix with the meat. Add the stock and wine, cover the pot, and braise over medium-low heat until the meat is tender, about 1 hour.

Meanwhile, heat the milk in a small saucepan set over medium-low heat and, when bubbling around the edges, add the butter and stir until it melts and is well mixed with the milk. Sprinkle the flour over the milk and stir until the béchamel is smooth. Set aside, covered, to keep warm.

Preheat the oven to 350°F.

When the meat is braised, add 2 or 3 tablespoons of the béchamel and the peas. Stir well to mix and form a creamy sauce. Add more béchamel if needed to round out the sauce and make it creamy and smooth, the perfect consistency for a pot pie filling. (Discard what you don't use.) Season with salt and pepper.

Transfer the pot pie filling to a 9-inch pie plate and spread evenly. Lay the crust over the filling and tuck its edges under the lip of the pie plate. With a small, sharp knife, make several slits in the crust. Brush the crust with melted butter and bake for 15 to 20 minutes, until the pie filling bubbles and the crust is golden brown.

Serve with Indian pickles and mango chutney.

SERVES 4 TO 6

2½ to 3 pounds trimmed, boneless goat roast, cut into 2-inch pieces

1 tablespoon Jamaican curry powder

Kosher salt

2 tablespoons vegetable oil

1 large yellow onion, diced

2 carrots, peeled and chopped

1 stalk celery, chopped

1½ cups chicken stock, preferably homemade

1 cup white wine

½ cup whole milk

1 tablespoon unsalted butter, plus a bit of melted butter for brushing the piecrust

1 tablespoon all-purpose flour

About ½ cup frozen peas (a good handful)

Freshly ground black pepper

One 10-inch round unbaked piecrust, homemade or store-bought

Indian pickles, for serving

Mango chutney, for serving

This recipe is so easy it's almost ridiculous. It could be the Irish-English in me who loves simply braised cabbage. And then, it could be the New Yorker in me who loves the idea of cabbage and caraway coming together (think about those towering deli sandwiches where cabbage and caraway inform a flavor backdrop over and over again). Finally, it's the adventurer in me who splashes passion fruit vinegar into the sauce. The result? Yeah, the dish works. Big time!

PORK TENDERLOIN WITH CABBAGE AND PASSION FRUIT MUSTARD

SERVES 4

2 pork tenderloins, 2 to 2½ pounds total

Kosher salt and freshly ground black pepper

4 tablespoons (½ stick) unsalted butter

1 clove garlic, minced

1 sprig fresh rosemary

2 small heads green or red cabbage, each halved and then each half halved again to make 8 wedges total

1 teaspoon caraway seeds, toasted (see Notes)

1 cup veal or chicken stock, preferably homemade (see Notes)

1 tablespoon passion fruit vinegar (see Notes) or another fruit vinegar

2 teaspoons Dijon mustard

Season the pork tenderloins with salt and pepper.

In a large skillet or sauté pan, melt 2 tablespoons of the butter over medium-high heat and, when bubbling, add the garlic and stir to mix, taking care that the garlic does not burn. Add the rosemary and the tenderloins. Cook the tenderloins, turning to brown lightly on all sides and basting with the buttery pan sauce, for 15 to 20 minutes. The pork is done when an instant-read thermometer inserted in the thickest part registers 145°F. Lift the pork tenderloins from the pan and set aside to rest for about 10 minutes. Cover the meat lightly with aluminum foil to keep it warm. Do not clean the skillet; set it aside with any pan juices still in it.

Meanwhile, put the cabbage wedges in a large saucepan and add 1 to 2 cups water, enough to come halfway up the cabbage. (You might need 2 saucepans, which is fine. Divide the caraway and butter between them.)

Add the caraway seeds and remaining 2 tablespoons butter and bring to a boil. Cover tightly, reduce the heat to medium, and cook until the cabbage is tender but still holds together, 7 to 10 minutes. Drain the pan and return the cabbage to it, covered, to keep warm.

Return the skillet with the reserved pan juices to the stove over medium heat. Add the stock and, when hot, add the vinegar and mustard and whisk until smooth and well mixed and any bits stuck to the bottom of the pan are incorporated into the sauce. Season to taste with salt and pepper.

To serve, slice the pork tenderloin and serve the cabbage alongside the pork. Drizzle the sauce over the meat and serve.

———

Notes: To toast caraway seeds, spread them in a dry skillet and toast over medium-high heat for 1 to 1½ minutes, until aromatic and they darken a shade or two. Slide the seeds onto a plate to cool.

Veal stock is naturally richer than chicken stock, so if you decide to use chicken stock, reduce it first to give it some body and concentrate its flavors. To do so, bring the stock to a boil in a saucepan, reduce the heat slightly, and simmer the stock rapidly until it reduces by half, 5 to 8 minutes. To ensure there is enough sauce, start with 1½ cups of chicken stock so that you end up with about ¾ cup.

I pretty much try every unusual or unfamiliar condiment I come across, which leads to some tasty finds, like passion fruit vinegar. The best known brand is A L'Olivier, which is made in France, but you can sometimes find similar vinegars made in small batches by specialty food companies. The vinegar is mixed with fruit pulp—most commonly passion fruit. The vinegar is expensive, no doubt about it, but once you try it, you'll be hooked and will want to splash it on fish and poultry, stir it into vinaigrettes, and add it to sauces.

Hey! Sometimes you just gotta do something funky, like wrap meat in hay. Get some clean hay from a nearby farm or a pumpkin patch and have some fun. I didn't make this up; it's a classic technique, and believe me, the hay will elevate the lamb's existing "barnyard-ness" in a tasty way. Go heavy on the rosemary and garlic, and, while you're at it, unscrew an Australian Shiraz. You're the cook, so pour yourself a glass.

LEG OF LAMB ROASTED
IN HAY WITH ROSEMARY AND GARLIC POTATOES

SERVES 6 TO 8

1 leg of lamb (8 to 9 pounds)

1 tablespoon dried oregano

Kosher salt and freshly ground black pepper

A good handful of clean, fresh hay

About 1 tablespoon date syrup (also called date honey)

Rosemary and Garlic Potatoes (page 201)

Preheat the oven to 325°F.

Season the leg of lamb with the oregano and salt and pepper. Set it on a rack in a roasting pan. Cover the lamb with the hay and then wrap the entire thing—roasting pan, hay, everything—in heavy-duty aluminum foil. Roast the aluminum foil–wrapped pan for 4½ to 5 hours.

Unwrap the pan and the lamb. Be sure to reserve the pan juices. Discard the hay.

Remove the rack with the lamb from the roasting pan so that you can pour the pan juices into a saucepan. Add the date syrup. Stir to mix. This will be the finishing glaze.

Turn on the broiler and, when hot, return the lamb to the roasting pan. Brush the lamb with the finishing glaze and broil the lamb for about 5 minutes to get a nice char.

Carve the lamb, drizzle with the finishing glaze, and serve with the Rosemary and Garlic Potatoes.

My mother-in-law is known for her yucca dishes, and I love both her and the yucca—the yucca mostly for its starchiness. Lightly mash it, and when you do, have an acidic vinaigrette, salsa verde, or pepper vinegar on hand to cut the starch. I serve it with oxtail, an inexpensive cut that is cherished by chefs for good reason: Its flavor is awesome. Don't fear it. If you want to freak out your dinner guests, serve the tail whole and uncut. And if you don't fancy the tail, substitute cubed top round of beef or another cut that works for stewing.

OXTAIL WITH
MASHED YUCCA

In a large glass, ceramic, or other nonreactive dish, whisk together the orange juice, olive oil, vinegar, garlic, cilantro, oregano, and coriander seeds. Put the oxtail into the marinade, stirring to make sure all the pieces are covered with marinade. Cover and refrigerate for at least 3 hours and up to 12 hours or overnight.

Preheat the oven to 325°F.

Remove the dish from the refrigerator, uncover it, and let it sit at room temperature for 20 to 30 minutes to take the chill off.

Transfer the contents of the dish to a deep pot; the marinade should nearly cover the oxtails and if not, add a little more juice. Cover with a lid and braise in the oven for 3 to 4 hours, until the meat is nearly falling off the bones. Alternatively, braise on top of the stove over medium-low heat for 2 to 3 hours.

Bring a large saucepan filled about two-thirds full with lightly salted water to a boil over high heat. Add the yucca and cook for about 30 minutes, or until softened and tender. Drain and return the soft yucca to the hot saucepan. Season with the granulated garlic and salt and pepper. Use a fork to mash it until smooth. Taste and adjust the seasonings if needed.

With a large slotted spoon, lift the oxtail from the pot and set on a platter, covered, to keep warm. Set the pot over high heat and bring the pan juices to a boil. Cook for a few minutes to reduce and thicken a little. Skim any fat from the surface.

Serve the oxtail spooned over the mashed yucca with the pan juices drizzled over it and the pepper vinegar on the side.

SERVES 6 TO 8

1½ cups orange juice

½ cup extra-virgin olive oil

¼ cup white wine vinegar

2 or 3 cloves garlic, chopped

1 sprig fresh cilantro, torn into a few pieces

1 tablespoon dried oregano

2 teaspoons coriander seeds

6 pounds oxtail, cut crosswise into 1-inch-thick pieces

3 pounds yucca root, scrubbed, peeled, and cut into 2- to 3-inch pieces

1 to 1½ teaspoons granulated garlic

Kosher salt and freshly ground black pepper

Pepper vinegar, for serving (see Note, page 126)

Three cheers for ham hocks—which are usually reserved for soup broth. Finally they're getting the attention they truly deserve. Slowly rehydrating them in gently simmering water allows them to recapture their sublime tenderness, which pairs just about perfectly with wilted greens, in particular somewhat spicy mustard greens. Ham hocks are smoky and salty and so impart a deliciousness to the braising water that is perfect for soup or cooking beans. You'll probably have to order the ham hocks, and if that's not convenient, make this recipe with slab bacon instead of the hocks.

SWEET-AND-SOUR
HAM HOCKS WITH MUSTARD GREENS

In a large pot, place the ham hocks, and pour enough cold water over them to cover by about 2 inches. Bring to a boil over high heat, reduce the heat, and simmer until tender, 3 to 4 hours. Adjust the heat up or down to maintain the simmer, and add more water as needed.

Meanwhile, in a large deep skillet, combine the vinegar with the sugar and bring to a simmer, stirring until the sugar dissolves. Add the capers and red pepper flakes and stir to mix. Finally, stir in the parsley.

Drain the ham hocks and toss them with the parsley sauce. Season to taste with salt.

Serve the ham hocks and the parsley sauce over the Mustard Greens.

SERVES 4

4 to 6 ham hocks

¾ cup white wine vinegar

3 tablespoons sugar

1 tablespoon drained capers

2 to 3 teaspoons crushed red pepper flakes

3 to 4 tablespoons chopped fresh flat-leaf parsley

Kosher salt

Mustard Greens (page 201)

I love this technique for prepping steaks, which I bastardized from my friends Alex Talbot and Aki Kamozawa, who write the blog *Ideas in Food*. It involves burying the steaks in blue cheese overnight to mimic the funk of dry aging. It works! For anyone with beer budgets and aged Bordeaux tastes, this is a godsend. Rib eye steaks are boned rib steaks, and one can be substituted for the other. I like them as thick as I can get them, so do your best to find hefty cuts. These are great with the Triple-Cooked Fries on page 201.

STEAK AND FRIES
WITH PICKLED ONIONS

SERVES 2

2 rib eye steaks, 1 to 1½ inches thick

1½ to 2 cups crumbled blue cheese

4 tablespoons (½ stick) unsalted butter, plus more for slathering (or the Snail Butter from *Try This at Home*)

16 to 20 cremini mushrooms, stems removed and caps left whole

½ cup seasoned rice vinegar

¼ cup soy sauce

1 tablespoon truffle oil

1 teaspoon grated fresh ginger

3 or 4 scallions, sliced, white and light green parts only

1 teaspoon garlic powder

Kosher salt and freshly ground black pepper

3 cloves garlic, smashed

2 sprigs fresh thyme

1 sprig fresh rosemary

Pickled Red Onions, for serving (page 217)

Put the steaks in a zipped plastic bag and pack the blue cheese around them. Push as much air as you can from the bag and zip it closed. Refrigerate the steaks for 12 hours or overnight.

In a large skillet set over medium-high heat, melt 1 tablespoon of the butter and, when bubbling hot, sear the mushrooms until golden brown, 4 to 5 minutes. In a glass mixing bowl, stir together the vinegar, soy sauce, truffle oil, and ginger. Add the scallions and browned mushrooms. Stir to mix and coat the mushrooms with the marinade. Set aside at room temperature while you prepare the steaks.

Remove the steaks from the bag and scrape off the blue cheese. Pat them dry with paper towels. Season both sides of the steaks with the garlic powder and salt and pepper and set them aside to come to room temperature.

Preheat the oven to 400°F.

Heat a large, heavy, oven-safe skillet—I like an old cast-iron pan with character—over medium-high heat and, when hot, melt the remaining 3 tablespoons butter. When the butter melts, add the smashed garlic, thyme, and rosemary. Stir these around a little, and then put the steaks in the pan. Cook the steaks for 3 minutes, and then turn over and cook for about 3 minutes on the other side, basting them with the melted butter as if you are in a race.

Transfer the skillet to the oven and cook for a few minutes longer, or until an instant-read thermometer inserted in a thick part of a steak registers 130° to 135°F. I insist on medium-pink meat with a touch of gray on the inside, and then nicely caramelized but not crunchy on the outside.

Let the meat rest for about 10 minutes. Slather more butter on the meat as it rests.

Serve the steaks with the veggies and Pickled Red Onions.

This is Italian simplicity at its finest, and that's saying *a lot*! You really want farmer's market or heritage pork here, and maybe some toasted sourdough for sopping up the roasting juices. The jammy anise condiment complements the crispy, fatty pork. And then there's the slightly bitter Swiss chard—my favorite quick-cooking green with just enough bite to counter the sweetish pork and jam.

PORCHETTA WITH FENNEL
MOSTARDA AND WILTED SWISS CHARD

SERVES 8 TO 10

One 7- to 8-pound boneless pork roast, butterflied so it lies sort of flat

Kosher salt and freshly ground black pepper

1½ pounds sweet Italian sausage, casings removed if necessary

2 tablespoons extra-virgin olive oil

2 cups diced fennel (about 1 medium fennel bulb)

½ cup white wine vinegar

¼ cup sugar

3 tablespoons mustard seeds

1 teaspoon mustard powder

2 bunches Swiss chard

2 cloves garlic, chopped

Piment d'Espelette or crushed red pepper flakes

Juice of ½ lemon

Lay the pork roast on a work surface and lightly season with salt and pepper. Spread the sausage meat over the pork and roll or fold the pork loin closed. Tie the porchetta with kitchen twine as you would any roast, making sure it's securely and tightly tied.

Preheat the oven to 325°F.

In a large skillet, heat the oil over medium-high heat. When very hot, sear the porchetta on all sides, turning it with tongs. Transfer to a rack set in a roasting pan and roast for about 3 hours, or until an instant-read thermometer registers higher than 155°F.

In a large saucepan, combine the fennel with the vinegar, sugar, mustard seeds, and mustard powder and bring to a boil over high heat. Reduce the heat to medium-low and simmer gently, stirring often and adjusting the heat to maintain the simmer, until the mixture is soft and syrupy and the fennel is nearly dissolved,

25 to 30 minutes. Set the mostarda aside, covered, to keep warm.

Lift the porchetta from the roasting pan and set aside to rest, loosely tented with aluminum foil to keep it warm.

Leave the Swiss chard leaves whole but cut out the base of the stems with a V cut. Rinse the chard and shake dry, leaving a little water clinging to the leaves.

Set the roasting pan, still with the pan juices, on a burner over medium heat, add the garlic and *piment d'Espelette*, and cook, stirring to blend. Add the Swiss chard and a squeeze of lemon juice and cook, stirring, until the chard wilts, about 15 minutes. Adjust the seasonings as needed.

Untie the porchetta and slice. Serve it with the Swiss chard and pass the mostarda at the table.

I know what you're thinking. A lamb's *head*? Yes. I gotta keep my street cred here, and believe me, it's traditional to make tacos with meat from hog jowls and ears, so why not a lamb's head? Unfortunately there's not as much meat on the head as needed to fill the tacos, so I've added a tail, which will nicely augment the meat supply. A nose-to-tail meal if ever there was one. (Though if you choose to use a leg of lamb, or lamb or pork shoulder, forget the tail.) If you tackle this with the lamb's head and post your results, I will follow you back on Instagram, Twitter, Snapchat, and Facebook. Wherever I can.

I like to serve this with as many different accompaniments as I can think of. In addition to the suggested salsa and radishes, try guacamole, cilantro leaves and stems, pickled carrots, pickled jalapeños, pickled onions, and cotija cheese.

BARBECUED LAMB'S HEAD
CARNITAS WITH MASA

Fill a bucket about two-thirds full with cold water. Add the salt, peppercorns, coriander seeds, and bay leaves. Submerge the lamb's head and the lamb's tail in the bucket and refrigerate, covered, for 2 days. If you haven't enough room in the fridge and it's cold outside, put the bucket in the garage or on a screened porch. The temperature of the air should hover around 41°F. (You can complete this step in a large bowl or even an oversize zipped plastic bag.) If you're using one of the alternative cuts of meat (the leg of lamb or pork shoulder), soak only for 24 hours.

Preheat the oven to 325°F.

Lift the lamb's head and tail from the bucket and rinse under cool running water. Pat dry with paper towels.

In a small bowl, whisk the olive oil with the orange juice. Add the cilantro, cumin, chile powder, and oregano and stir well. Brush the marinade over the meat and season with salt and pepper.

Wrap the head and tail in several layers of aluminum foil, put it in a roasting pan, and roast for 5 hours, or until the meat is cooked through and an instant-read thermometer registers 140°F for lamb and 150°F for pork.

Meanwhile, in a large mixing bowl, stir the masa harina with 1 cup warm water until smooth and well mixed. Set aside to rest for about 30 minutes.

In a deep, heavy pot, heat the lard (you will need a depth of 3-plus inches) over high heat until it registers 375°F on a deep-frying thermometer.

Form the masa into golf ball–size pieces and then flatten into cakes. Using long-handled tongs, submerge a cake in the hot lard and fry for a few minutes, until puffy. Lift the puffed cake from the lard and drain on a paper towel–lined baking sheet. Using a spoon, immediately depress the center of the hot masa cake to create a taco shape. Repeat with the remaining masa to make about 24 tacos.

SERVES 4 TO 6

2 handfuls of kosher salt

10 whole black peppercorns

Small handful of coriander seeds

2 or 3 bay leaves

1 lamb's head or 2- to 2½-pound leg of lamb or lamb or pork shoulder (see Note)

1 lamb's tail (see Note)

½ cup extra-virgin olive oil

¼ cup orange juice

2 tablespoons chopped fresh cilantro

1 teaspoon ground cumin

1 teaspoon ancho chile powder

1 teaspoon dried oregano

Freshly ground black pepper

1½ pounds masa harina

About 1½ pounds manteca (lard), or about 3 cups vegetable oil

Mild salsa (your favorite kind), for serving

Sliced fresh radishes, for serving

Unwrap the lamb and capture the accumulated juices in a bowl. Strain the juices into a saucepan. Skim as much fat from the juices as possible and then bring to a simmer over medium-high heat. Cook for about 5 minutes to reduce the pan juices just a little.

Slice the meat and serve with the tacos, reduced pan juices, salsa, and radishes.

Note: You may have to order a lamb's head and tail from the butcher. The head should weigh about 3 pounds, and the tail should weigh 2 to 3 pounds. You'll have to ask the butcher to clean out the eye sockets. The lamb's head won't have as much meat as the leg of lamb or the pork shoulder; most will come from the cheeks, plus the tail will add more meat to the dish.

I've been spending a lot of time in Hawaii lately and so I present this dish without apology. It's got "family picnic" or "take-to-church casserole" written all over it, especially if you live on the islands (or dream of living there). Don't hesitate to punch up the rice with a little sambal. The natural sweetness of the pineapple more than stands up to it.

PORK BELLY CHAR SUI
WITH PINEAPPLE FRIED RICE

To make the pork belly, in a glass, ceramic, or other nonreactive bowl, stir together the soy sauce, honey, hoisin, oyster sauce, garlic, and ginger. Add a few drops of organic food coloring, if using.

Lay the belly in a large glass dish or similar container and pour the marinade over it. Turn a few times to make sure the meat is covered with marinade. Cover the dish. (Alternatively, put the belly in a large, zipped plastic bag and pour the marinade over it. Slosh the meat around in the marinade.) Refrigerate the pork belly for 3 to 4 hours and up to 12 hours or overnight, turning a few times.

Preheat the oven to 325°F.

Lift the pork belly from the marinade, letting the excess drip back into the dish. Wrap the meat in three layers of aluminum foil, folding it so that no cooking juices will be able to escape. Lay the foil package on a baking sheet and roast for 4½ to 5 hours.

Holding the package over a pan, unwrap the pork belly. Allow the juices to drain into the pan. Skim and blot as much fat from the juices as possible. Set the pan over high heat and bring the pan juices to a boil. Lower the heat and simmer until the juices reduce by about one-third, 6 to 7 minutes. Cover to keep warm, and set aside. Before serving, skim any fat that rises to the surface.

Turn on the broiler and, when hot, broil the pork belly on the baking sheet, fat side up, for about 5 minutes to give it a nice char. Set aside.

To make the fried rice, in a large cast-iron skillet or wok, heat the sesame oil over medium-high heat until smoking. Add the rice and eggs and stir to coat the rice with egg and oil. Immediately add the garlic and ginger and stir to mix, taking care that the garlic does not burn. Fold in the scallions and pineapple. Stir in the soy sauce and season to taste with vinegar.

Reduce the heat to medium and keep stirring the rice. When heated through, it's ready to be served.

Slice the pork belly and serve with the fried rice. Pass the reduced pan juices at the table.

SERVES 6 TO 8

PORK BELLY

2 cups soy sauce

½ cup honey

¼ cup hoisin sauce

2 tablespoons oyster sauce

3 cloves garlic, chopped

2-inch knob fresh ginger, peeled and shredded

2 or 3 drops organic red food coloring or beet juice (optional)

One 3-pound slab pork belly, about 12 inches long

FRIED RICE

3 tablespoons sesame oil

3 to 4 cups cooked and cooled white rice, preferably 1 day old

2 large eggs, lightly beaten

1 clove garlic, finely chopped

1-inch knob fresh ginger, peeled and chopped

4 scallions, diced, white and light green parts only

1 cup diced pineapple (about 8 ounces; I like drained canned pineapple rings for this)

2 to 3 teaspoons soy sauce

Mushroom or rice vinegar, for seasoning

My homage to the British tradition of serving thick slices of roast beef with horseradish cream omits the Yorkshire pudding but includes kale. The greens grab more than a hint of licorice from star anise, which then bumps up against the nutmeg with an almost palate-numbing thump.

ROAST BEAST DINNER
WITH LICORICE KALE AND HORSERADISH

SERVES 8 TO 10

About ¾ cup lightly packed dark or light brown sugar

3 to 4 tablespoons yellow (ballpark) mustard

1 tablespoon coriander seeds

2 to 3 teaspoons garlic powder

One 4- to 4½-pound boneless rump roast, first-cut brisket, or bone-in short ribs

Kosher salt and freshly ground black pepper

½ cup whole milk

1 tablespoon unsalted butter

1 tablespoon all-purpose flour

1 large bunch kale, stems trimmed and ribs removed

2 tablespoons extra-virgin olive oil

1 clove garlic, minced

2 teaspoons crushed red pepper flakes

2 star anise

About ½ cup prepared creamy horseradish

Preheat the oven to 325°F.

In a mixing bowl, mix together the brown sugar and mustard until it is the consistency of wet sand.

Rub the coriander seeds and garlic powder over the meat on all sides. Season lightly with salt and pepper. Set the roast in the center of a large sheet of aluminum foil and rub it with the brown sugar mixture, covering it as thoroughly as possible. Wrap the roast with the foil, taking care to close any gaps. Wrap the meat in two or three more sheets of foil so that it is securely covered with no room for leaks.

Set the wrapped meat in a roasting pan and roast for 5½ hours. Shortly before the roast is done, heat the milk in a small saucepan set over medium-low heat. When bubbling around the edges, add the butter and stir until it melts and is well mixed with the milk. Sprinkle the flour over the milk and stir until the béchamel is smooth. Set aside, covered, to keep warm.

Slice the trimmed kale leaves into thin strips. Rinse them under cool water and shake dry so that a little water clings to them.

In a large skillet, heat the olive oil over medium heat. When hot, add the garlic and red pepper flakes and stir to start them cooking. Add the kale and cook, stirring, until wilted and tender. Add the béchamel and star anise, stir well, and simmer, stirring occasionally, for 15 minutes longer.

Unwrap the roast, making sure to capture the pan juices. Set the roast on a carving board for about 15 minutes to rest. Meanwhile, skim any fat from the pan juices and then cook them over medium-high heat to reduce just a little.

Carve the roast and serve it with the kale, horseradish, and reduced pan juices.

Bone. In. Hamburger. Need I say more? It's magnificent in design and a little curious in its parody, which makes it a natural for some retro fried spuds like tater tots. Go ahead and buy them if you want—they're one of the few processed foods that cannot be matched by artisan attempts, regardless how earnest. Don't forget to toss the tots with salt and chopped parsley before serving. Visual window dressing and bold flavor.

BONE-IN SALISBURY
STEAK WITH TATER TOTS AND CHERRY KETCHUP

Using a box grater or the grater of a food processor, grate the potato. Put the grated potato in a bowl and mix with the egg white, nutmeg, and salt and pepper. Lay a sheet of plastic wrap on the work surface and scrape the potato mixture into the center. Roll the potato mixture into a cylinder, using the plastic wrap as a guide. Freeze for at least 2 hours and up to 12 hours or overnight.

In a small bowl, stir the ketchup with the jam. Add the Worcestershire sauce and stir well. Set aside.

In a mixing bowl, use your hands to mix together the chuck, brisket, and short rib meat. Season the meat with salt and pepper and form into a 12-ounce patty. Lay the caul fat on the work surface and put the patty in the center. Position the bones next to the meat and wrap it tightly in the caul fat.

Pour the oil into a deep skillet to a depth of 2 to 3 inches. Heat over medium-high heat until the oil registers 360°F on a deep-frying thermometer.

Meanwhile, unwrap the potato cylinder and cut the frozen mixture into disks, each about ½ inch thick.

When the oil is hot, add the still frozen or barely thawed tater tots and fry, turning once, until golden brown, 2 to 3 minutes; do not crowd the pan, and let the oil regain its temperature between batches. Drain the tots on paper towels. Transfer to a bowl and toss the hot tots with salt and the parsley.

In a large skillet (I recommend a cast-iron skillet), melt the butter over medium-high heat. Add the garlic, rosemary, and thyme and then cook the patty for 3 to 4 minutes on each side for medium-rare.

Unwrap the patty from the caul fat and remove the bones. Serve with the tater tots and pass the ketchup on the side.

Note: Don't let caul fat scare you. It's lightweight and easy to work with, sold in sheets from high-end butchers and online. It is the fat that surrounds the internal organs of the steer (and other animals). It's also called lace or netting fat because of its webbed pattern. Because it's thin and relatively light, it's often used for sausage casing and to cover pâtés. Sorry to say, there is no substitute for it—so this is the exception to my rule of supplying alternatives for hard-to-find ingredients.

SERVES 2

1 large or 2 medium russet potatoes, peeled

1 large egg white

1 teaspoon ground nutmeg

Kosher salt and freshly ground black pepper

¾ cup ketchup

¾ cup sour cherry jam or preserves

Dash of Worcestershire sauce

4 ounces ground chuck

4 ounces ground brisket

4 ounces ground short rib beef (if you can't find this, increase the amounts of chuck and brisket by 2 ounces each)

1 piece caul fat, about the size of a large baking sheet (see Note)

2 rib eye bones, cleaned (ask the butcher)

Vegetable oil, for frying

2 to 3 tablespoons chopped fresh flat-leaf parsley

2 tablespoons unsalted butter (I like to use clarified butter)

1 clove garlic, finely chopped

1 sprig fresh rosemary, leaves chopped

1 sprig fresh thyme, leaves chopped

I used to be embarrassed by my love for sweet-and-sour dishes. What a cliché! Another American drawn to an "exotic dish" that is cloyingly sweet. But I'm over it. Now I'm openly enthusiastic about sweet-and-sour food, and nothing figures into the sweet part of the equation as deliciously as pineapple. I love pineapple like McDonald's founder Ray Kroc loved pineapple. Back in the 1960s, he introduced the Hula Burger, a pineapple slice with cheese on a bun. It flopped, but you gotta admire the guy for trying! The key to any sweet-and-sour dish is balance—make sure there's enough vinegar and enough pineapple, but not too much of one or the other. Simple enough?

PORK CHEEKS
AND PINEAPPLE

Season the pork with salt and pepper. In a heavy, deep pot with a tight-fitting lid, heat the oil over high heat. When hot, sear the pork, turning several times to brown on all sides; you might have to do this in batches so as not to crowd the pot. Remove the pork from the pot and set aside.

Add the onions, reduce the heat to medium-high, and cook, stirring, until soft and translucent, 6 to 7 minutes. Add the garlic, cilantro stems, Thai chiles, and star anise and cook, stirring, until fragrant, 2 to 3 minutes. Stir the tomato puree into the pot until well mixed.

Return the pork and any accumulated juices to the pot and stir to mix well. Add the stock and fish sauce and cook for a few minutes to heat the liquid. Slowly add the pineapple and its syrup, stirring carefully so the cubes don't mush it all up. Add the vinegar and stir to mix.

Cover the pot with the lid and braise over medium-low heat until the meat is cooked through but not dry, 1 to 1½ hours.

Season to taste with salt and pepper and ladle the stew into shallow bowls. Garnish each bowl with the cilantro leaves.

SERVES 4

- 2 pounds pork cheeks or boneless pork shoulder, cut into 1½- to 2-inch chunks
- Kosher salt and freshly ground black pepper
- 2 tablespoons grapeseed oil
- 2 yellow onions, chopped (about 2 cups)
- 2 cloves garlic, minced
- Leaves from 1 bunch fresh cilantro, stems reserved
- 2 Thai chiles, seeded and minced
- 3 star anise
- 2 tablespoons tomato puree
- 1 quart pork, veal, or chicken stock, preferably homemade
- 2 tablespoons Thai fish sauce
- One 15-ounce can diced pineapple in syrup
- ½ cup white wine vinegar

The last time I was in Hong Kong, I was blown away by the noodle bowls that included dumplings. And I've always applauded the Chinese love affair with off-cuts of meat, which is why I champion trotters (pigs' feet) here. Succulent, sticky, sweet, and all porcine, they are close to irreplaceable. That said, I won't be miffed if the pigs' feet morph into chicken thighs in your house. I love those, too, and so will this dish.

HONG KONG BOWL WITH
TROTTERS AND WONTONS

In a heavy pot with a tight-fitting lid, place the trotters and cover with the stock and vermouth. If necessary, add more stock or some water to make sure the meat is covered by 1 to 2 inches. Add the onions, carrots, and celery and stir to mix. Season lightly with salt and pepper. Bring to a boil over high heat, reduce the heat to medium, and cover the pot. Simmer gently until the meat is so tender it just about falls off the bone, about 4 hours. Check often and adjust the heat to maintain the simmer.

Meanwhile, chop the shrimp into very small pieces and put in a mixing bowl. Add the scallions, soy sauce, vinegar, oil, ginger, and garlic. Season lightly with salt and pepper. Mix well, cover, and refrigerate for at least 1 hour and up to 12 hours or overnight.

Lay a few wonton wrappers on a work surface and put 1 teaspoon of the filling in the center of each one. Brush a little egg on the edges of each wrapper and then pull the edges up and over the filling. Pinch the edges together to make a secure bundle. Repeat with the remaining wonton wrappers and filling. As they are folded, put the wontons on a baking sheet and dust them very lightly with cornstarch. (If you have leftover filling, use it to make more wontons or fry it up and have a party for yourself!)

Fill a large saucepan filled about two-thirds full with lightly salted water and bring to a boil. Add the ramen noodles and cook until al dente, 2 to 3 minutes. Drain and return the noodles to the hot pan. Cover to keep warm.

Lift the trotters from the braising broth and set aside. Skim as much fat as you can from the broth and then season the remaining broth with salt. Bring the sauce to a simmer over medium heat and add the dumplings. Let them cook until heated through, about 2 minutes. Lift them from the broth, and then add the bok choy. Return the trotters to the pot and cook for about 5 minutes or until the bok choy wilts and everything is piping-hot.

Divide the ramen among shallow bowls and top each with a trotter. Add a few bok choy leaves and 3 wontons to each bowl. Ladle the broth over the trotters. Serve immediately.

―――――

Note: Trotters are pigs' feet and are beloved by many. They can be front or back feet and typically are pickled or smoked, although they're also braised. Buy whole feet that haven't been split and rinse them under cool running water. You might have to special-order them from a butcher.

SERVES 6

6 trotters (see Note)

2 cups pork or chicken stock, preferably homemade

½ cup dry vermouth

1 yellow onion, chopped (about 1 cup)

1 carrot, peeled and chopped

1 stalk celery, chopped

Kosher salt and freshly ground black pepper

8 ounces large shrimp, peeled and deveined

2 or 3 scallions, finely chopped, white and light green parts only (about ⅓ cup)

2 teaspoons soy sauce

1 teaspoon rice wine vinegar

2 teaspoons dark sesame oil

½-inch knob fresh ginger, peeled and chopped

1 clove garlic, minced

18 wonton wrappers, 3 inches in diameter

1 large egg, lightly beaten

Cornstarch, for dusting

1 pound ramen noodles

½ large head bok choy, ribs cut from the bottom of each leaf

VEGETABLE

I cook vegetarian dishes from a carnivore's perspective, which means I imagine trying to convince someone who likes a bloody rib eye that he'll be very happy with one of these recipes on Meatless Monday or any other day of the week.

I don't think it would take much persuasion. These dishes are bursting with big, bold, assertive, confident flavors that make skipping meat a few times a week just fine. Heck, it's good for our health, our world, and our pocketbooks, and so why not? My wife teaches yoga and my kids are growing up in hip Southern California and so we sometimes joke that we're a meal away from being vegan. These dishes don't go that far, but they are the convincers: as far from bland, steamed veggies as you can get. The paella is unmistakably paella, with saffron and wine and so many other flavors that no one will miss the seafood or sausages. The gutsy beet loaf has the texture of meat loaf; the grain bowl has so many flavors and textures, your head will spin. You get the idea.

Give me a break! The recipe's title is punny. I love puns. But seriously, the loaf is tasty, filling, and bursting with healthfulness, the kind of meal you might end up making once a week. If you do, expect requests for seconds, even from meat lovers. You might want to work with the ratios of veg until you achieve the perfect "meat-like" texture for your taste, but even the results of the tinkering will be delicious. You'll need a meat grinder for this veg dish.

VEGETARIAN BEET LOAF

Preheat the oven to 350°F.

Put the beets and oats in an 8- or 9-inch square baking pan, add about ½ cup water, season lightly with salt and pepper, and stir to mix. Cover tightly with aluminum foil or a lid and roast the beets for about 1 hour or until easily pierced with a fork. Let the beets cool until you can handle them. Slip the skins off the beets and cut into large chunks.

Meanwhile, pour water into a large saucepan to a depth of about 1 inch. Add the cauliflower, season lightly with salt and pepper, cover tightly, and bring to a boil over high heat. Reduce the heat and simmer until fork-tender, about 15 minutes. Drain and set aside until needed.

In a meat grinder fitted with a large-hole plate, grind the beets, mushrooms, and hazelnuts so they are coarsely chopped. Alternatively, use a food processor fitted with the metal blade, but take care not to overprocess; the mixture should be chunky and textured.

In a large sauté pan, heat the oil over medium-high heat. Add the onions and garlic and cook, stirring, until the onions begin to soften, 2 to 3 minutes. Take care that the garlic does not burn. Add the carrot and cook, stirring, until barely fork-tender, about 10 minutes. Add the ground veggie mixture, the cauliflower, and the Montreal seasoning and stir to mix. Season to taste with salt and pepper. Stir in the barley and quinoa and, when well mixed, transfer the mixture to a rigid plastic container with a tight-fitting lid or similar container. Let the mixture cool, and then refrigerate, tightly covered, for about 2 hours. The goal is to chill the mixture.

When chilled, transfer the mixture to a large mixing bowl and add the egg, egg yolk, and parsley. Mix well, and then spoon the mixture into a 6-cup terrine mold (or a 9-by-5-by-3-inch loaf pan or similar pan). Push the mixture into the mold so that it fills the corners, and smooth the top. Wrap the terrine mold with plastic wrap and weight the top with cans of food (such as tomatoes or beans) or another weight. Refrigerate the weighted terrine for 12 hours or overnight.

Preheat the oven to 350°F.

Unwrap the terrine mold and bake for about 45 minutes or until the loaf is hot in the center. In a small bowl, whisk together the tomato paste and honey. During the last few minutes of baking, brush this over the top of the loaf. Serve hot.

Note: You don't have to use Montreal steak seasoning. Instead, use one of your particular favorites. I like the one made by McCormick; it's in every supermarket in the land, and it adds good flavor. Steak seasonings generally are mixtures of garlic and onion powder, paprika, crushed red pepper flakes, and salt and pepper. Depending on the brand, they might include coriander or dill.

SERVES 6 TO 8

1 pound beets (8 to 10), trimmed

¼ cup rolled oats

Kosher salt and freshly ground black pepper

1 small head cauliflower, separated into small florets

1 pound portobello mushrooms, coarsely chopped

8 ounces hazelnuts (about ¾ cup)

2 tablespoons extra-virgin olive oil

1 small yellow onion, minced (¾ to 1 cup)

2 or 3 cloves garlic, minced

1 carrot, trimmed, peeled, and diced (about ½ cup)

3 tablespoons Montreal steak seasoning (see Note)

1 cup cooked barley

1 cup cooked quinoa

1 large egg

1 large egg yolk

½ cup chopped fresh flat-leaf parsley

½ cup tomato paste

3 tablespoons honey

By now you know how much I appreciate a good pun. But more to the point, any time I can riff on a traditionally meat-based dish with a plant-based one, I'm there. While the deep red hue of the beets might have you thinking of red meat, it's the overall depth of flavor that will keep the chili purists out there—and you know who you are!—nodding their heads in approval.

BEET AND BARLEY CHILI

Put the beets and mushrooms through a meat grinder until finely ground. Alternatively, grind the beets and mushrooms in the bowl of a food processor fitted with the metal blade. Set aside.

In a deep, heavy pot, heat the oil over medium-high heat. When hot, reduce the heat to medium, add the onions, carrots, and peppers, and cook, stirring, until the vegetables start to soften, about 5 minutes. Add the garlic and cook, stirring, for 1 or 2 minutes, and then stir in the barley.

Add the oregano and chili powder and season to taste with salt. Stir to mix well, then add the ground beets and mushrooms and mix well.

Add the stock and wine, scraping the bottom of the pot with a wooden spoon to dislodge any browned bits. Raise the heat and bring to a boil. Reduce the heat and simmer for about 15 minutes.

Add the kidney and black beans and cook over medium-high heat, stirring occasionally, until the chili is very hot, 10 to 15 minutes.

Adjust the seasoning with more chili powder and salt, as necessary. Stir in the vinegar, molasses, and cumin, then taste and adjust the seasonings again.

Ladle into shallow bowls and top with the cilantro. Serve with yogurt, cheese, and hot sauce.

SERVES 6 TO 8

About 8 ounces beets (5 or 6 beets), peeled

1 pound white button mushrooms, stemmed and coarsely chopped (about 2 cups)

2 tablespoons vegetable oil

1 yellow onion, chopped (about 1 cup)

1 large carrot, chopped (about ½ cup)

1 red bell pepper, seeded and chopped

1 green bell pepper, seeded and chopped

6 cloves garlic, chopped

1 cup barley

2 to 3 tablespoons dried oregano

1 tablespoon chili powder

Kosher salt

1 quart vegetable or chicken stock, preferably homemade

Splash of red wine or red wine vinegar

One 15-ounce can kidney beans, drained

One 15-ounce can black beans, drained

3 to 4 tablespoons balsamic vinegar

About 1 tablespoon molasses

1 to 2 teaspoons ground cumin

2 to 3 tablespoons chopped fresh cilantro

Plain whole-milk Greek yogurt, for serving

Crumbled cotija cheese, queso fresco, or feta cheese, for serving

Hot pepper sauce, for serving

My wife, Jazmin, is a yoga instructor and a most-of-the-time vegetarian. She doesn't complain when I cook meat for dinner, so this is one way I make it up to her. A savory, warm, hearty dish that doesn't miss anything.

CHICKPEAS AND POTATOES WITH MASHED LENTILS

SERVES 4

2 tablespoons ghee or unsalted butter

½ yellow onion, finely chopped

1 teaspoon grated garlic

1 teaspoon grated fresh ginger

Pinch of crushed red pepper flakes

1 cup halved fingerling potatoes (about 3 small potatoes)

One 16-ounce can chickpeas, drained

1½ cups vegetable stock, preferably homemade

1 teaspoon fenugreek powder

1 teaspoon ground turmeric

1½ cups green or brown lentils

1 teaspoon garam masala

Kosher salt

2 to 3 teaspoons chopped fresh cilantro

1 to 2 teaspoons chopped fresh mint leaves

1 or 2 squeezes fresh lemon or lime juice

1 cup plain whole-milk Greek yogurt

Indian pickles, for garnish (optional)

In a large cast-iron skillet, heat the ghee until hot. Add the onions, garlic, ginger, and red pepper flakes and cook over medium-high heat, stirring, until the onions soften, 3 to 4 minutes.

Add the potatoes to the skillet and cook, stirring, until they start to soften, about 10 minutes. Add the chickpeas, 1 cup of the vegetable stock, the fenugreek, and turmeric. Reduce the heat to medium and cook, stirring occasionally, until the potatoes are cooked through and the liquid is reduced by about half, 8 to 10 minutes.

In a saucepan, combine the lentils with the remaining ½ cup vegetable stock and ½ cup water. Add the garam masala and season to taste with salt. Bring to a boil over medium-high heat, then reduce the heat and simmer gently until the lentils are soft, 25 to 30 minutes.

At this point, you can puree the lentils in a blender until smooth and fold them into the potatoes. Otherwise, stir the lentils and their liquid into the potato mixture.

Garnish with the cilantro and mint and a squeeze or two of lemon juice. Serve with yogurt dolloped on top and some Indian pickles on the side, if using.

Here's a vegetarian dish that's actually "meaty." I have fond memories of straining gigantic cauldrons of veal stock when I was a young apprentice chef. It was physically hard work—and so usually foisted on the young, who couldn't say no. Of course, in truth those "fond memories" are of snacking on the soft, tender carrots that had simmered for hours and hours with the veal bones. I re-created that taste and texture sensation as a veg dish centered around colossal carrots (the kind you feed to horses).

HORSE CARROT
POT ROAST

Cut the green tops off the carrots and reserve. Wash the carrots but don't peel them. Cut them into 2-inch-long lengths.

In a sauté pan or skillet, heat the vegetable oil over medium-high heat. Sear the carrots, turning until they start to brown, 3 to 4 minutes. Add the smashed garlic, bay leaf, and peppercorns and cook, stirring, for about 1 minute. Add the wine and stir with a wooden spoon to scrape up any browned bits sticking to the pan.

Add the onions, sugar, and tomato paste, reduce the heat to medium-low, and cook gently until the carrots are incredibly tender and the wine sauce is close to syrupy, 25 to 30 minutes.

Fill a saucepan about two-thirds full with lightly salted cold water. Add the potatoes, bring to a boil over medium-high heat, and lower the heat. Simmer rapidly until the potatoes are fork-tender, 15 to 18 minutes.

Meanwhile, heat the cream over medium heat until hot but not boiling.

Drain the potatoes, reserving the cooking water to cook the carrot tops. Return the potatoes to the empty hot saucepan. Add the hot cream and the butter and mash until smooth. Season to taste with salt and pepper.

Pour the reserved potato cooking water into a large skillet and bring to a simmer over medium heat. Add the reserved carrot tops and blanch just until softened, 2 to 3 minutes. Drain.

Finely chop the blanched carrot tops and transfer to a small mixing bowl. Add the parsley, mint, olive oil, lemon juice, and grated garlic. Stir to mix.

Spoon the potatoes into a casserole or a decorative dish. Top with the carrot pot roast mixture. Drizzle the carrot top and herb mixture over the carrots. Garnish the pot roast with the thyme sprigs and onion flowers, if using, and serve.

4 very large carrots, with carrot tops

1 tablespoon vegetable oil

4 to 6 cloves garlic, smashed

1 bay leaf

5 or 6 whole black peppercorns

1½ cups Zinfandel (half of a 750 ml bottle)

About 1 cup pearl onions, peeled (I toss in a handful)

2 tablespoons sugar

2 tablespoons tomato paste

3 or 4 Yukon Gold potatoes, peeled and cut into large chunks

½ cup heavy cream

3 tablespoons unsalted butter

Kosher salt and freshly ground white pepper

¼ cup chopped fresh flat-leaf parsley

1 teaspoon chopped fresh mint leaves

About 1 tablespoon extra-virgin olive oil

Juice of ½ lemon

1 clove garlic, grated

1 or 2 sprigs fresh thyme

Onion flowers, for garnish (optional)

Here's a vegetarian dish that's filling without being heavy. Eggplant has always been a good substitute for meat, in part because it's naturally fleshly—which I love, because *fleshy* is a fun word to type and to say. There are a lot of textures going on here, but not much fat. A dish that's healthful *and* that you can throw together in about half an hour.

CHARRED EGGPLANT
WITH CHICKPEAS, OLIVES, AND ZA'ATAR-SPIKED YOGURT

Preheat the broiler or prepare a gas or charcoal grill so that the heating elements or coals are hot.

Char the whole eggplants for 5 to 6 minutes or longer, turning them so that they are somewhat charred and blistered on all sides. Remove the eggplants from the broiler or grill and let them cool slightly.

Split the eggplants in half lengthwise and set on the countertop, cut sides up. Season each eggplant half lightly with salt and pepper and then drizzle with olive oil. Scatter each with cilantro and then a squeeze of lemon juice.

Meanwhile, put the chickpeas and their liquid in a saucepan. Add about 1/4 cup water and about 1 tablespoon of the za'atar. Heat over medium-high heat and, when heated through, season to taste with salt. Remove the chickpeas from the heat and add the olives and capers. Stir to mix. Add the orange segments and mix gently.

In a small bowl, mix the yogurt with the remaining 1 tablespoon za'atar. Taste and add more if desired.

Spoon some yogurt on each plate. Top with 4 eggplant halves and some chickpeas. Garnish with parsley, toasted pine nuts, and dandelion leaves or arugula, if using.

———

Notes: Za'atar is a Middle Eastern spice mix composed of sumac and sesame seeds as well as herbs. There are slight variations among different suppliers but all share a similar warm, aromatic flavor profile.

To toast pine nuts, spread them in a dry skillet and toast over medium-high heat until they darken by two or three shades and are lightly browned, 4 to 6 minutes. Shake the pan often during toasting to prevent sticking. Slide the pine nuts from the skillet onto a plate to cool completely.

SERVES 6

12 Japanese eggplants

Kosher salt and freshly ground black pepper

About 1/4 cup extra-virgin olive oil

2 tablespoons chopped fresh cilantro

1/2 lemon

One 16-ounce can chickpeas, not drained

2 tablespoons za'atar spice mix (see Notes)

1/4 cup sliced pitted green olives

1 tablespoon drained capers

2 oranges, peeled and divided into segments

1 1/2 cups plain whole-milk Greek yogurt

Fresh flat-leaf parsley, for garnish

Pine nuts, toasted, for garnish (see Notes)

Dandelion leaves or arugula, for garnish (optional)

Paella is all about rice and saffron, and once these are mastered, you won't miss the seafood and meat that usually show up in more traditional paellas. Go big on the garlic, herbs, and saffron, and you'll find yourself questioning why paella ever needed seafood or sausage in the first place.

VEGETABLE PAELLA

SERVES 4

In a paella pan or large cast-iron pot, heat the olive oil over medium-high heat. When hot, add the onions, celery, and bell pepper. Cook, stirring, until the vegetables begin to soften, about 3 minutes. Add the garlic and cook, stirring, for another minute or so, until the vegetables are aromatic.

Stir in the rice and spice mix and then stir in the eggplant. Add the wine and saffron and stir gently to mix. Cook until the wine starts to reduce and the alcohol cooks off, 4 to 5 minutes.

Add the stock. There should be enough stock to cover the rice by ½ inch. If there's not, add a little more. Reduce the heat to medium and let the mixture cook undisturbed until the rice is cooked and the liquid evaporates, 20 to 25 minutes. At this point, the bottom of the rice will stick to the pan and be lightly browned.

During the last few minutes of cooking, stir in the chard, piquillo peppers, parsley, and caperberries and let them cook until heated. Add the vinegar, stir well, and, when the paella is hot, taste and add salt, if needed. Serve the paella directly from the pan.

Notes: Paella rice makes a difference when you cook paella. If you can't find Bomba rice, which is considered by many to be the best rice for paella, use any medium-grain rice, such as Valencia. For more on rice, see opposite.

Paella spice mix generally contains saffron, paprika, cayenne, garlic powder, salt, and pepper, as well as other ingredients such as dried parsley and roasted bell peppers, depending on the brand. You can find it online and in most supermarkets and specialty shops.

2 tablespoons extra-virgin olive oil

¼ cup finely diced yellow onion (about ¼ onion)

½ stalk celery, finely diced (about ¼ cup)

¼ green bell pepper, finely diced (about ¼ cup)

4 large cloves garlic, thinly sliced (about ¼ cup)

1 pound Bomba paella rice (see Notes)

¼ cup paella spice mix (see Notes)

3 to 4 ounces eggplant (about ¼ of a purple globe eggplant), sliced into half-moons

¼ cup white wine

Pinch of saffron

2 to 3 cups vegetable stock, preferably homemade (enough to cover the rice by ½ inch)

2 or 3 Swiss chard leaves, torn (about 1 loosely packed cup)

¼ cup drained and chopped jarred piquillo peppers

¼ cup chopped fresh flat-leaf parsley (about ½ bunch)

Handful of jarred caperberries, stemmed and halved

2 tablespoons sherry vinegar

Kosher salt

Rice, Rice Baby . . .

When I was a boy, I thought all rice was white and served alongside the main course in place of potatoes, because who can eat potatoes every day? Okay, let's be honest, when I was a boy, I never thought about rice. I ate it, but that's about it.

Now I am a man, and rice is a pretty big part of my life. I appreciate its versatility and how healthful it is. I make a mean congee (see the Chinese Chicken and Rice Porridge on page 76) and an irresistible risotto (see the English Pea Risotto on page 194). What I've learned about rice is that, just as there are different pastas for different dishes, there are some varieties of rice that work better for some dishes than others. And yet, as is the case with pasta, you won't ruin the dish if you—oh, no!—use the *wrong* rice.

More people on the planet eat rice than any other grain, and over the years, centuries really, farmers and cooks have conspired to develop strains that work best with the region's cooking style. (Or is it the other way around? The rice determined the cooking style? A chicken-and-egg conundrum if ever there was one!)

For example, sushi rice is either medium- or short-grain, and because of this and how it's cooked, is sticky. Risotto is best made with a medium-grain rice grown in Northern Italy with a high starch content. During cooking, the starch dissolves in the hot liquid and helps the rice develop its desirable creaminess. Examples of risotto rice are Arborio, Carnaroli, and Vialone Nano. Indian and Pakistani dishes are frequently made with basmati rice, a highly aromatic long-grain rice, while the dishes of Southeast Asia often call for floral-scented jasmine rice. And then there's paella from Spain, which is served with a medium-grain rice that stands up to all the other ingredients in that robust dish.

White rice, the kind I ate as a boy, is long-grain rice that has been milled to remove the hull and the bran. Brown rice has not been so milled and the hull is intact. Because of this, brown rice takes a little longer to cook and supplies more nutrients.

The rice that grows in the American South (and elsewhere in the world) is long-grain rice, and when it's cooked it separates into fluffy white grains. This sort of rice is used for all sorts of dishes, such as pilafs and casseroles.

I could continue. There's black rice, glutinous rice, instant rice, converted rice, red rice, pecan rice, wild rice, and oh-I-don't-know! It's an awesome grain and one you'll see used a lot in these pages.

Chock-full, ingredient-layered bowls run rampant in trendy California. They're everywhere, although I'm not sure if they've conquered the rest of the country. If the concept is new to you, I guarantee this bowl will become your fave go-to lunch. Piled with grains, condiments, and pickles, it's kind of a grain-ular salad bar in a bowl. And if you have leftovers, they can be reborn in another bowl tomorrow.

EGG-TOPPED HERITAGE
GRAIN BOWL

In a large skillet or wok, heat the oil over high heat. When hot, add the cooked grains, garlic, ginger, and scallions and stir-fry until the vegetables soften and the grains are hot, 5 to 7 minutes. Add the soy sauce and vinegar and stir just to mix and heat.

Meanwhile, in a saucepan filled about halfway with water, submerge the eggs. Bring to a boil, reduce the heat to a rapid simmer, and cook the eggs for exactly 6 minutes from the time the water started boiling. Drain.

Divide the hot grains among shallow bowls. Top each with a cracked soft-boiled egg, some avocado, pickled onions, mustard caviar, and cilantro. Add the cooked chicken and/or bacon, if using. Serve immediately.

SERVES 6

2 tablespoons peanut oil

½ cup cooked quinoa

½ cup cooked farro

¼ cup cooked amaranth

¼ cup cooked Kamut

2 cloves garlic, minced

1-inch knob fresh ginger, peeled and chopped

2 or 3 scallions, chopped, white and light green parts only

Splash of soy sauce

Splash of brown rice vinegar or rice vinegar

6 large eggs

2 ripe avocados, pitted, peeled, and chopped or cut into wedges

1 cup Pickled Red Onions (page 217)

About 1½ tablespoons mustard caviar (pickled mustard seeds) or grainy mustard

2 tablespoons chopped fresh cilantro

About 2 cups chopped cooked chicken (optional)

3 or 4 slices bacon, cooked and broken into pieces (optional)

A simple bag of frozen peas used in two different ways informs this risotto, the Rolls-Royce of rice dishes. So elegant and yet not difficult, unless you are trying to make it on a cooking competition show! Serve this as the main event or make it a side. Together, let's bring risotto back, people!

ENGLISH PEA RISOTTO

SERVES 4

One 1-pound bag frozen peas

4 tablespoons (½ stick) unsalted butter, at room temperature

2 quarts vegetable stock, preferably homemade

1 tablespoon extra-virgin olive oil

1 yellow onion, minced

1 clove garlic, minced

2 cups Carnaroli or Arborio rice

Kosher salt and freshly ground white pepper

3 to 3½ ounces Parmesan cheese, grated or shaved

Juice of ½ lemon

2 to 3 tablespoons chopped fresh flat-leaf parsley (I use what I call a baby's handful)

About 2 teaspoons chopped fresh mint leaves

In a deep saucepan, bring about 1 inch of water to a boil. Blanch the peas just until thawed and beginning to soften, about 1 minute. Drain the peas and set half of them aside to use later. Transfer the other half to the canister of a blender. Pulse until the peas form a smooth puree. Scrape the puree from the blender into a lidded container. Chill for at least 1 hour and up to 12 hours or overnight.

Remove the pea puree from the container and blend with the softened butter. Work the butter and peas with a rubber spatula or wooden spoon until very well mixed.

In a pot, heat the broth. In a large saucepan, heat the oil over medium-high heat and, when hot, add the onion and garlic and cook, stirring, until the onion softens, 2 to 3 minutes. Add the rice and stir for a minute or two, until the rice starts to smell nutty. Add ½ cup of the hot broth and cook, stirring, until the broth is absorbed by the rice.

Set the pot holding the hot broth near the pot with the rice and pour a ladle of broth into the rice. Stir after each addition, making sure the liquid is absorbed before adding the next ladleful. This process will take 18 to 20 minutes (maybe longer), and at the end the rice will be cooked through and richly creamy; all the broth will be absorbed. (You may not use every last drop of the broth; use your best judgment.)

Season the risotto with salt and pepper and then stir in a generous ¼ cup of the pea butter. Stir over medium heat until it is well integrated into the risotto. Taste and add a little more of the pea butter, if desired. Fold the reserved blanched peas and the Parmesan into the risotto. When mixed and hot all the way through, stir in the lemon juice, parsley, and mint. Serve the risotto right away.

ON THE SIDE

I am all about side dishes. At Thanksgiving, I'm crazier about the veg and starch than the turkey; I think my record is 15 sides at one Thanksgiving dinner! When I eat out, I look first at the sides and the apps on the menu. I never fail to order side dishes, too, knowing that while they are great upsales for restaurants (an easy way to clear a few bucks), they also encourage creativity in the kitchen. They make the meal, if you ask me. End of story.

Something about the fusion of fragrant rosemary and pungent garlic can't be beat. And the potatoes seal the deal.

ROSEMARY
AND GARLIC POTATOES

SERVES 6 TO 8

3 to 3½ pounds small round potatoes (look for the smallest you can find so that you can keep them whole)

3 tablespoons unsalted butter

3 sprigs fresh rosemary, leaves chopped

1 large bunch fresh flat-leaf parsley, leaves chopped

2 cloves garlic, minced

Salt and freshly ground black pepper

Set a roasting pan on a burner. Add the potatoes and butter to the pan and cook over medium-high heat, rolling the potatoes around and coating them with butter as the potatoes cook and the butter melts. After 25 to 30 minutes, the potatoes will be brown, slightly shriveled, and cooked through.

Add the rosemary, parsley, and garlic and toss with the hot, buttery potatoes. Season to taste with salt and pepper, and serve hot or warm.

You can cook any green—mustard, chard, kale, spinach—this way. I like to use butter, but switch to olive oil, if you prefer. Or mix them. Wilting greens is so easy, so quick, and the result is always satisfying.

MUSTARD
GREENS

SERVES 4

2 tablespoons unsalted butter

2 cloves garlic, minced

2 bunches mustard greens (about 3 pounds), stems trimmed

Kosher salt and freshly ground black pepper

In a large skillet, melt the butter over medium heat. Add the garlic and the rinsed but not dried greens; there should be some water clinging to the leaves. Cook, stirring, until the greens wilt, about 15 minutes. Season to taste with salt and pepper and serve immediately.

As much as I love french fries, onion rings are my go-to, and a bit more of a chef's choice. This recipe has evolved over the years, and these days I like to use a whip canister to deliver a lighter-than-air batter to coat the onions. A few years ago, I'd have to describe a whip canister in detail, but now I can say it's what they use at your favorite coffee shop to dispense the whipped cream. They're easily sourced online or can be bought in your favorite kitchen supply shop. Serve these with ketchup mixed with a little kimchi for a mega crave-worthy umami bomb.

ONION RINGS

Pour the oil into a deep, heavy pot to reach a depth of 3 to 3½ inches, or pour the oil into a deep-fat fryer. Heat the oil over high heat until it reaches 350°F on a deep-frying thermometer.

Meanwhile, in a mixing bowl, toss 1 cup of the flour with the cornstarch. Season lightly with salt and pepper and whisk to mix. Add the seltzer and stir to mix well to make a tempura batter.

Pour the tempura batter into a whip canister and charge it with 2 cream (nitrous) charges. Discharge the batter into a clean, dry mixing bowl. The batter should be light and airy. Alternatively, whisk the batter well after adding the seltzer so that it's light and frothy.

Pour the buttermilk into one shallow bowl and spread the remaining 1 cup flour in another. Season the flour with salt and pepper.

Dip the onion rings first in the buttermilk and then in the flour. Knock off the excess flour and dip the onion rings in the tempura batter.

Gently submerge the coated onions, a few at a time, in the hot oil and fry until golden brown and crispy, 3 to 4 minutes. Lift the onion rings from the hot oil with a slotted spoon and drain on paper towels. Lightly season with salt while still warm.

Proceed with the remaining onion rings. Be sure the oil regains its temperature between batches. Serve the onion rings while still warm.

SERVES 4

Vegetable oil, for frying

2 cups all-purpose flour

1 tablespoon cornstarch

Kosher salt and freshly ground black pepper

1½ cups seltzer

2 cups 1% or 2% buttermilk

2 yellow onions, sliced into ¼-inch-thick rings

This simple side dish is popular at one of my restaurants and is a great study in contrasts. The sweet, charred, crunchy snap peas play nicely with the salty, briny, crumbly feta.

SNAP PEAS WITH
FETA AND MINT

In a mixing bowl, stir the mayonnaise with the paprika and all but 1 tablespoon of the lemon juice. Cover and refrigerate the aioli for up to 12 hours, or set aside to use very soon. If it is refrigerated, let it warm up to cool room temperature before using.

Heat a large skillet over high heat. When hot, pour in the oil. Add the snap peas and blister for about 30 seconds to char on one side. Turn over and char for about 30 seconds on the other side.

Toss the snap peas with the aioli and mint. Serve topped with the feta and drizzled with the reserved 1 tablespoon lemon juice.

_____

Note: To make your own mayonnaise for the aioli, put 2 large egg yolks, the paprika, and the lemon juice in a blender. With the motor running, pour about 4 cups olive oil into the pitcher, blending until the mixture emulsifies to a mayo-like consistency. Season to taste with salt.

SERVES 6

3 cups mayonnaise
(see Note)

¼ cup hot paprika

Juice of 1 lemon

2 tablespoons canola oil

2 pounds snap peas, trimmed

½ cup loosely packed
fresh mint leaves

1 cup crumbled feta cheese

I've been cooking—and eating—french fries since I was a baby and pretty much enjoying every bite. With that pedigree, I feel I can proclaim with 100 percent certainty that following this process makes a truly *great* fry! I urge you to try frying them in the beef or duck fat I suggest (see more about them in the Note at the end of the recipe). Don't let the type of fat put you off—particularly because the fat pretty much makes the fry. I start the spuds in water, which preps them for the subsequent fryings. The double frying and the chilling create a light brown canvas of crevasses and fissures that, after two plunges into hot fat, produce irresistibly crunchy, crackly french fries. I've talked enough; I'm hungry!

TRIPLE-COOKED FRIES

Cut the potatoes into strips approximately ½ to ¾ inch wide and ½ inch thick. As you cut them, submerge them in a bowl filled with cold water to prevent oxidizing (turning color).

Fill a stockpot with cold water, add a little salt, and bring to a boil over medium-high heat.

Lift the potatoes from the cold water with a slotted spoon and cook in the boiling water until fork-tender, 10 to 12 minutes. Lift the potatoes from the water and spread out on a paper towel–lined baking sheet. Pat the potatoes dry, replace the original layer of paper towels with dry paper towels, and refrigerate for at least 15 minutes.

Meanwhile, in a deep, heavy pot or deep-fat fryer, bring the fat to a temperature of 275°F over medium-high heat.

Working in batches, fry the chilled potatoes for 3 to 5 minutes before lifting them from the hot oil with a slotted metal spoon and spreading on the baking sheet (no paper towels this time!). Let the oil regain its heat between batches. Chill the potatoes again for about 15 minutes.

While the potatoes chill, raise the heat under the fat or adjust the thermostat on the fryer and heat the fat to 375°F.

Fry the chilled potatoes again until golden brown and crispy, 4 to 5 minutes, working in batches and letting the fat regain its heat between each one. Use tongs or extra-long chopsticks to break the potatoes apart, if necessary, and turn them in the fat so that they brown evenly.

With a slotted spoon, transfer the fries to a shallow bowl. Add the parsley and toss to mix. Season with salt and serve warm.

———

Note: If you can get beef or duck fat, you won't be sorry. The flavor either one imparts is impossible to match. You'll probably have to work with a butcher or beg a local restaurant chef to help you secure your gallon of fat, but in the end you'll be happy. On the other hand, these fries are damn good when fried in a vegetable oil with a high smoking point, such as canola, soy, or sunflower oil.

SERVES 4

5 pounds russet potatoes, peeled

Kosher salt

1 gallon beef tallow or duck fat (see Note)

1 bunch fresh flat-leaf parsley, chopped

I have dreams of being an outdoorsman or even a survivalist. If the TV show *Naked and Afraid* comes calling, I'll bring the can of beans. These appeal to my taste for sweet and sour. And they're about the best baked beans I've tasted. You'll agree!

CAMPFIRE
BAKED BEANS

Put the beans in a large bowl and cover with cold water. Let the beans soak for at least 6 hours and up to 12 hours or overnight.

Drain and transfer the beans to a saucepan. Add enough cold water to the pan to cover the beans by 1 to 2 inches and bring to a boil over high heat. Reduce the heat, skim any foam that rises to the surface, and simmer until the beans are tender, 1 to 1½ hours; adjust the heat up or down to maintain the simmer and add more water only as needed to keep the beans covered.

Add the molasses, ketchup, mustard, and paprika to the beans and their cooking liquid and stir to mix. Add a splash of Worcestershire sauce and cook over medium heat, stirring, until the ingredients are well mixed and heated through, 10 to 15 minutes. (Alternatively, mix the cooked beans with your favorite barbecue sauce.)

SERVES 4

2 cups dried pinto beans

¼ cup molasses

¼ cup ketchup

2 tablespoons Dijon mustard

2 teaspoons smoked paprika

Splash of Worcestershire sauce

Celery roots look gnarly and ugly, but they taste earthy, nutty, and sweet. I like to cook them simply with cream and a little salt and pepper. Although they taste a little like celery, they aren't the root of the familiar stalk celery—so don't run to your garden and start digging.

CELERY ROOT
PUREE

SERVES 4 TO 6

2 celery roots (celeriac), peeled and coarsely chopped

2 cups heavy cream

Kosher salt and freshly ground black pepper

Put the celery root in a deep skillet and pour the cream over it. Set the pan over medium heat and, when the cream bubbles around the edges of the pan, season to taste with salt and pepper. Continue simmering the celery root until tender when pierced with a fork, 25 to 30 minutes.

With a slotted spoon, lift the celery root from the cream and transfer to a blender or the bowl of a food processor fitted with the metal blade. Add about 2 tablespoons of the hot cream and puree until smooth. Alternatively, mash the celery root with a fork, adding a little cream as needed. Serve warm.

If you like, you can puree the celery root ahead of time and reheat it gently before serving. You might want to add a little cream when you reheat.

This is a holiday favorite at my house and it is so easy it almost doesn't need a recipe: Cook rutabagas until tender and mash them with sweet butter. *Finis!* Oh, yeah: Salt and pepper, please.

MASHED
RUTABAGAS

Fill a large pot about two-thirds full with cold water. Sprinkle with salt and bring to a boil over high heat. Add the rutabagas, reduce the heat to medium-high, and cook until tender, about 20 minutes; the cooking time will depend on how large the pieces of rutabaga are.

Drain and then mash the rutabagas with the butter until almost smooth (this is not a puree, but rather is meant to be rustic). Season to taste with salt and pepper. Serve warm.

SERVES 6 TO 8

Kosher salt

4 rutabagas, peeled and chopped into pieces

2 tablespoons unsalted butter

Freshly ground black pepper

This recipe for super-tender biscuits comes from a long line of Southern biscuit bakers, although none were from my family. I stumbled on the method while working with food scientist—and Southerner—Shirley Corriher. Imitation is the best form of flattery; thank you, Shirley!

BUTTERMILK
BISCUITS

Preheat the oven to 425°F.

In a large mixing bowl, whisk the self-rising flour with the sugar and salt. Add the butter, working it into the flour with your fingers until it resembles coarse meal.

Slowly add the cream, mixing it gently with the flour using a wooden spoon and your fingers. Gradually add the buttermilk. Watch the consistency of the batter, which should be loose and clumped, similar to cottage cheese, but wetter and messier (not soupy).

Sprinkle some of the all-purpose flour over a baking sheet.

Divide the batter into 8 pieces—you can eyeball this. Scoop a piece into your hand and sprinkle with enough all-purpose flour to keep it from sticking to your hands as you shape it into a round biscuit. Put the biscuits on the baking sheet, positioning them so that they touch each other.

Bake for 20 to 25 minutes, until the tops are golden brown. Brush with the melted butter and serve hot.

MAKES ABOUT 8 PALM-SIZE BISCUITS

2 cups self-rising flour

¼ cup sugar

½ teaspoon salt

4 tablespoons (½ stick) unsalted butter or vegetable shortening (such as Crisco), cut into pieces and chilled

⅔ cup heavy cream

1 cup 1% or 2% buttermilk

About 1 cup all-purpose flour

3 tablespoons unsalted butter, melted

When I lived in the South, it took me a while to appreciate many of the traditional dishes. Not so with corn bread! The natural sweetness of the corn, boosted with a little added sugar, makes this a great sponge for any salty or spicy dish, from barbecue to vinegary braised greens. Or serve it as it comes from the oven: still warm and crunchy and maybe with a pat of sweet butter. I like to use blue cornmeal, but if you want to use up that bag of white or yellow cornmeal in your pantry, go for it!

SOUTHERN-STYLE
CORN BREAD

Preheat the oven to 375°F. Line the bottom of a 10-inch round cake pan with parchment or wax paper. Brush the sides of the pan with a little melted butter.

In a small bowl, mash the room-temperature butter with the jalapeño until well mixed. Season with a little salt and set aside. You want the butter to be soft when it's served with the warm cornbread, so don't refrigerate it until you've used as much as you need. It will keep in the refrigerator for up to 1 week.

In a mixing bowl, whisk together the cornmeal, flour, baking powder, sugar, and 2 teaspoons salt.

In another bowl, whisk together the eggs, milk, and melted butter. When blended, slowly add the wet ingredients to the dry ingredients and stir until thoroughly mixed. Do not overmix.

Pour the batter into the prepared pan and bake for about 20 minutes or until a toothpick or small knife inserted in the center comes out clean.

Set the corn bread, still in the pan, on a wire rack to cool until just warm. Cut and serve with the jalapeño butter.

SERVES 4 TO 6; MAKES ONE 10-INCH CAKE

1 pound (4 sticks) unsalted butter, at room temperature

1 jalapeño, seeded and diced

Salt

1⅓ cups blue cornmeal

1 cup plus 2 tablespoons all-purpose flour

1½ tablespoons baking powder

1 tablespoon sugar

4 large eggs

2 cups whole milk, at room temperature

1 cup (2 sticks) unsalted butter, melted and cooled

You Better Believe It's Butter!

If you've read through the recipes on these pages and those in my previous book, *Try This at Home*, you know I like butter. Slathered on hot biscuits and corn bread, stirred into pan sauces, used to sauté onions and garlic . . . nothing beats fresh, creamy butter. Of course olive oil and other oils are great for cooking, too, but there are times when nothing will do but butter.

Ever since mankind has been milking cows, goats, sheep, and yaks, they've been separating the cream from the milk and then agitating it to separate the fat solids from the liquid (that liquid is called buttermilk). What's left behind is butter. When I call for butter, I mean the stuff made from cow's milk, which I'm sure is your definition as well.

Most butter sold in the United States is sold by the pound, separated into neatly wrapped, 4-ounce sticks. European butters show up with increasing frequency on our supermarket shelves, and while more expensive than familiar brands—often richer and creamier, too—they are generally packaged in blocks. Local U.S. creameries offer butters with similar profiles to European brands—and similar price tags. Some of these are sold in large markets, although you're more likely to find them in specialty shops and farmer's markets. Keep an eye out!

Butter is 80 to 85 percent milk fat, with American stick butter weighing in at 80 to 81 percent and high-quality European and domestic brands at 83 to 85 percent fat. (The rest of the butter is naturally occurring liquid.) Slightly higher fat contents make the butter richer, smoother, and creamier, although butters with lower fat contents work very well for most cooking and baking needs.

Butter is perishable and picks up strong odors. Because of this, keep it wrapped and stored in the fridge away from pungent foods like onions, fish, and cheese. It keeps in the refrigerator for about two months if salted and, if unsalted, for about half that time. Salted or not, butter freezes beautifully for up to six months—good news for anyone who likes to bake in the middle of the night and needs that butter to make cake batter or cookie dough.

When I drop a few chunky pats of butter in a sauté pan, I wait until it melts and bubbles. As soon as the bubbling starts to diminish, I add the food. It works.

If you've never tried fried pickles, or even heard of them, I'm sad for you. But now you can welcome them into your life, so I'd argue that buying this book was worth it just for this page! I like to make my own pickles, but when I can't and I'm feeling it, I find that those ridged dill slices sold in jars or any bread-and-butter pickles fry up fine. Best of all, I make tempura batter for the pickles (and for the onion rings on page 203)—it's one of my all-time favorites. I'd dip just about anything in this light and airy batter and then fry it for perfect crunch: pickles, onions, broccoli, Oreos.

SOUTHERN FRIED
PICKLES

Slice the cucumbers into rounds ¼ to ½ inch thick and put in a large bowl. Sprinkle generously with salt and set aside to allow the salt to draw the water from the cukes.

Meanwhile, in a large pot, combine the vinegar, both sugars, mustard seeds, and turmeric and bring to a boil over medium-high heat. Boil for a few minutes, or until the sugar dissolves. Remove from the heat.

Transfer the cucumbers to a large colander and rinse under cool running water to remove the salt. Put the rinsed cukes in a large glass, ceramic, or other nonreactive bowl and pour the pickling liquid over them. Set aside to soak for about 30 minutes.

Meanwhile, pour the oil into a deep, heavy pot or deep-fat fryer so that it's three-quarters full and heat over medium-high heat until it registers 350°F on a deep-frying thermometer.

While the oil heats, in a mixing bowl, toss 1 cup of the flour with the cornstarch. Add the seltzer and stir to mix well to make a tempura batter.

Pour the tempura batter into a whip canister and charge it with 2 cream (nitrous) charges.

Discharge the batter into a clean, dry mixing bowl. The batter should be light and airy. Alternatively, whisk the batter well after adding the seltzer so that it's light and frothy.

Spread the remaining 1 cup of flour in a shallow bowl. Lift the pickles from the brine and dip in the flour. Knock off the excess flour and dip the pickles in the tempura batter.

Gently submerge the coated pickles, a few at a time, in the hot oil and fry until golden brown and crispy, 3 to 4 minutes. Lift the pickles from the hot oil with a slotted spoon and drain on paper towels. Season lightly with salt. Proceed with the remaining pickles. Be sure the oil regains its temperature between batches. Serve the pickles while still warm.

———

Note: This recipe makes a lot of brine, more than you'll need for a pound of cucumbers. But why not make a lot? This way you can pickle more cukes right away, or something else when the mood strikes. Keep the brine in a tightly lidded glass jar for up to 2 weeks. And of course, you can cut the brine amount in half if that better suits your needs.

SERVES 4 OR MORE

About 1 pound cucumbers (2 or 3 cukes)

Kosher salt

1 gallon apple cider vinegar

4 cups granulated sugar

4 cups packed light brown sugar

¼ cup yellow mustard seeds

¼ cup ground turmeric

Vegetable oil, for frying

2 cups all-purpose flour

1 tablespoon cornstarch

1½ cups seltzer

I always have these in the refrigerator. They go well on sandwiches, salads, roasted meat, really anything.

PICKLED
RED ONIONS

MAKES ABOUT ½ CUP

1 cup white vinegar

½ cup sugar

½ red onion, thinly sliced

In a small saucepan, bring the vinegar and sugar to a boil over medium-high heat. Put the red onion slices in a small glass bowl and pour the hot liquid over them. Set aside to steep and cool for at least 1 hour.

The pickled onions and their brine will keep in a lidded container in the refrigerator for at least 2 weeks. (I prefer glass containers for pickles.)

Use these just about any time you need bread crumbs. Easy to make and will keep for a week or so in the fridge. Once you've made your own crumbs, you won't want buy those stale-tasting, commercially produced crumbs. Sawdust. No thanks.

SEASONED
BREAD CRUMBS

MAKES A SCANT 1¼ CUPS

2 or 3 good-size slices slightly stale sourdough bread or baguette

1 tablespoon chopped fresh flat-leaf parsley

1 tablespoon garlic powder

1 tablespoon grated lemon zest

1 teaspoon kosher salt

1 teaspoon freshly ground black pepper

Preheat the oven to 350°F.

Lay the bread slices on a baking sheet and toast for about 8 minutes, turning once, or until golden brown. (Alternatively, use a toaster.) Crush the bread into coarse crumbs with your hands, a blender, or a food processor and transfer to a medium bowl. You should have about 1 cup of crumbs.

Add the parsley, garlic powder, lemon zest, salt, and pepper. Toss to combine evenly.

Store the bread crumbs in a tightly lidded container in the refrigerator for up to 2 weeks.

DESSERTS

They say no one gets angry at bartenders and pastry chefs. Who doesn't enjoy a cocktail or a dessert now and then? And so, here are some of my favorite desserts (hold the cocktails). Keep in mind that I'm not a pastry chef and so the recipes here are more rustic, more family friendly than the picture-perfect, modern plated desserts we offer at my restaurant Juniper and Ivy. These are just right for home cooking.

I like dessert. I don't have a massive sweet tooth but enjoy a good sweet. And I believe in indulgence. You don't want to eat dessert every day, but when you want cheesecake, have a real cheesecake. When you want caramel sauce, make it authentic. Don't go overboard with the sugar, but you need enough to wake up the other flavors. Follow the recipe—this isn't the place to improvise until you understand what's going on. Think about it: Ice cream, crème anglaise, and panna cotta are essentially eggs, milk (cream), and sugar. How these ingredients are handled determines the texture and flavor of the final product—and makes them quite different from one another. And so much about desserts is about texture: smooth, creamy, chunky, crunchy, crackling. . . .

I can't deny that desserts have interested me more as my kids have been growing up. I mean, who can resist the joy of handing someone an ice cream cone? Smiles all around.

Barley with dessert? Why not? Infusing cream with toasted, malted barley gives this beloved Italian dessert a nuance that is indescribably tasty. I know panna cotta may seem like a lot of work, but don't worry: I simplified the recipe, and I know you can do it. Don't let barley down!

BARLEY PANNA COTTA
WITH COFFEE CRÈME ANGLAISE

SERVES 4 TO 6

1 quart heavy cream

½ cup sugar

1 teaspoon kosher salt

1 cup barley malt, or 1 cup regular barley plus 3 tablespoons vanilla malt powder (see Note)

6 tablespoons gelatin (3 ounces)

About 1 cup Coffee Crème Anglaise (opposite)

Spray four to six 8-ounce custard cups or ramekins with flavorless vegetable spray.

In a saucepan, combine the cream, sugar, and salt and cook, stirring, over medium heat until the sugar dissolves and the cream is hot. Remove the pan from the heat and stir in the barley malt. Cover and set aside for 30 minutes to give the barley malt time to flavor the cream.

Meanwhile, add about 9 tablespoons cold water to a small bowl. Sprinkle the gelatin over the water as evenly as you can and let it soak for 5 to 10 minutes, until softened and squishy.

Pour the cream through a fine-mesh sieve into another saucepan. Discard the barley malt. Set the pan over low heat and cook for a few minutes, just until warm. Pour the warm cream over the gelatin and stir until the gelatin is completely dissolved. Let the mixture cool to room temperature.

Pour the panna cotta into the prepared custard cups and refrigerate for at least 2 hours and up to 12 hours or overnight, until set.

To unmold, run a sharp knife around the rim of each cup and invert onto a small plate. Spoon generous amounts of the Coffee Crème Anglaise over each panna cotta. (Alternatively, pour the panna cotta mixture into cognac snifters or other decorative glasses. This way you can serve the dessert without unmolding, thus lessening the waiting time and labor.)

Note: Barley that has been "malted" is called barley malt. Any grain can be malted, a process that encourages germination before halting it at a point where certain enzymes convert starches to sugar. Dried barley malt is sold in many supermarkets and natural food stores, as well as online. It's not expensive, but if you prefer, for this recipe mix regular barley with vanilla malt powder, available at the same outlets as barley malt.

The panna cotta on the opposite page is completed with a few spoonfuls of this sauce, yet it's a stand-alone recipe for a smooth custard sauce that works equally well spooned over ice cream . . . cake . . . berries. . . .

COFFEE CRÈME
ANGLAISE

In a small bowl, whisk the egg yolks with 2 tablespoons of the sugar until smooth.

In a saucepan, whisk together the cream, milk, the remaining 2 tablespoons sugar, the coffee granules, cornstarch, and vanilla and heat over medium-high heat until boiling.

Pour about ¼ cup of the hot liquid over the egg yolks and whisk briskly to incorporate. Stir in the rest of the cream mixture and whisk well. Strain the custard through a fine-mesh strainer into a bowl.

Submerge the bowl in a larger bowl filled with cold water and ice and let it chill; the ice bath chills the custard more quickly than the refrigerator. Stir occasionally to speed up the chilling.

Serve immediately, or cover and refrigerate for up to 1 week.

MAKES ABOUT 2 CUPS

2 large egg yolks

4 tablespoons sugar

1 cup heavy cream

1 cup whole milk

2 tablespoons instant coffee granules or powder

2 teaspoons cornstarch

1 teaspoon pure vanilla extract

Everyone loves cheesecake, and why not? The gentle emulsion of brown sugar and cream cheese whipped to ethereal peaks is a surefire way to put off those dieting plans for another day. I'm so fond of the sinfully rich stuff, I've asked interns to walk from lower Manhattan across the Brooklyn Bridge and a few blocks into Brooklyn—and back again—to fetch me a slice of Junior's world famous cheesecake. You gotta pay your dues, right? Oh, wait. That wasn't me, it was Sean "Puffy" Combs. But you get the point. Good cheesecake is good enough to turn anyone into a horrible boss.

BROWN SUGAR CHEESECAKE IN OREO CRUST WITH HONEYED BLUEBERRIES

Put the cookies in a zipped plastic bag and expel as much air as you can. Lay the bag on a work surface and roll a heavy rolling pin over it. Keep rolling until the cookies form fine crumbs.

Transfer the crumbs to a mixing bowl and add the melted butter. Stir the crumbs until they are moistened with the butter. Press the crumbs into a 12-inch springform pan, pressing them across the bottom and a little bit up the sides.

Preheat the oven to 325°F.

In the bowl of an electric mixer fitted with the paddle attachment, beat the cream cheese on low speed until smooth. Scrape down the sides of the bowl occasionally. Add the sugar, cinnamon, and vanilla and mix until well incorporated, smooth, and light.

Add the eggs, one at a time, mixing well after each addition and continuing to scrape down the sides of the bowl. Pour the mixture into the prepared springform pan and smooth the surface.

Wrap the bottom and up the sides of the springform pan with aluminum foil. Set the pan in a roasting pan and set it on an oven rack.

Pour enough warm water into the roasting pan to come halfway up the sides of the springform pan.

Bake the cheesecake for 1 to 1½ hours, until it's set around the edges. Remove the springform pan from the roasting pan, discard the foil, and let the cheesecake cool in the springform pan set on a wire rack for at least 2 hours or until barely warm.

Refrigerate for at least 2 hours and for as long as 12 hours or overnight. When chilled, release the sides of the springform pan and serve the cheesecake on the springform's base. Spoon the Honeyed Blueberries over the cake for serving.

———

Note: Just for fun, I like to take the cheesecake to the next level—and then some. Here's how: Break up the cooled cheesecake and stuff it in the bowl of a food processor fitted with the metal blade. Pulse until the cheesecake turns into crumbles. Put the crumbles in a 1-quart whip canister. Charge twice with a nitrous cream charger. Shake vigorously after each charge and use as needed. For example, squirt it directly into your mouth!

SERVES 10 TO 12; MAKES ONE 12-INCH CHEESECAKE

20 Oreo cookies

½ cup (1 stick) butter, melted

24 ounces (three 8-ounce packages) cream cheese, softened

1 cup lightly packed light brown sugar

1 teaspoon ground cinnamon

½ teaspoon pure vanilla extract

3 large eggs

Honeyed Blueberries (page 226)

Slightly sweetened blueberries are not necessarily expected with cheesecake, but you'll be glad they came. Spoon these over ice cream or cake, too.

HONEYED
BLUEBERRIES

MAKES ABOUT 1 CUP

1 cup fresh blueberries

¼ cup honey

¼ cup water

In a small saucepan, combine the blueberries with the honey and water. Bring to a simmer over medium heat and cook until the mixture thickens slightly, 2 to 3 minutes. The blueberries are ready when the syrup coats the back of a spoon. Remove from the heat and spoon over the cheesecake.

The blueberries can be made ahead of time, refrigerated, and then reheated over low heat. If needed, add a little more water when reheating.

A delicious way to get your kids to eat avocados. And one with just enough sweetness to surprise and charm the adults in the crowd.

AVOCADO
TOASTS

SERVES 6

8 avocados, pitted and peeled

1 cup unsweetened cocoa powder

⅓ cup honey

6 thick slices sourdough bread

3 pints raspberries or strawberries

Put the avocados, cocoa powder, and honey in the bowl of a food processor fitted with the metal blade. Blend until smooth.

Toast (or grill) the bread slices until golden brown.

Spread the avocado puree over the toasts and then top with the berries. Serve right away.

Bread pudding is the go-to recipe for any chef who tends to prepare savory dishes far more often than dessert. If you find yourself competing on a cooking show and need to whip up a warm dessert, bread pudding is a star. I sometimes think of bread pudding as holiday stuffing, with the cream replacing the turkey stock. The key to making it your own is to keep it simple and remember that its success lies with the bread. Here, I up the luxury quotient with crusty, buttery, sugary croissants. Buy a few extra because, believe me, you'll have trouble resisting them while letting them dry out.

HEATH BAR CHOCOLATE
BREAD PUDDING

Preheat the oven to 350°F and butter a 9-inch round cake pan.

Arrange the croissant pieces on a rimmed baking sheet and toast in the oven for about 10 minutes, or until lightly browned. Transfer to the buttered pan. Turn off the oven.

In a mixing bowl, whisk together the eggs, ½ cup of the milk, ½ cup of the sugar, the Bailey's, and cocoa until the sugar begins to dissolve. Set aside.

In a large saucepan, whisk the remaining 2 cups milk with the remaining 1 cup sugar. Add 1½ cups of the heavy cream and heat over medium heat, stirring, until the sugar dissolves; do not let the mixture boil. Remove the mixture from the heat.

Whisking the egg mixture constantly, slowly pour about ½ cup of the hot milk mixture into it. Whisk until smooth. Pour the tempered egg mixture into the saucepan holding the warm cream.

Heat the custard over medium heat, stirring constantly with a wooden spoon. Maintain a low simmer and cook until the custard is thick enough to coat the back of the wooden spoon and leaves an obvious trail when you draw a finger through it, 5 to 6 minutes.

Pour the custard over the croissants, making sure the bread is completely submerged. Cover with plastic wrap and refrigerate for about 1 hour to chill the custard so that the pudding appears set.

Preheat the oven to 300°F.

Scatter the toffee bits over the pudding and stir to mix. Bake for 55 to 60 minutes, until the custard sets and the top is golden brown.

Let the pudding cool so that it's not piping-hot.

Meanwhile, in the chilled bowl of an electric mixer, beat the remaining 1 cup heavy cream on medium-high speed until thick. Add the confectioners' sugar and continue to beat until the cream forms soft peaks when the beaters are lifted from the bowl, 1 to 2 minutes longer.

Serve the pudding warm with the whipped cream on the side.

**SERVES 6 TO 8;
MAKES ONE 9-INCH
ROUND PUDDING**

10 or 11 day-old croissants, broken into ½-inch pieces

8 large eggs

2½ cups whole milk

1½ cups sugar

3 tablespoons Bailey's Original Irish Cream

2 tablespoons unsweetened cocoa powder

2½ cups heavy cream

1½ cups Heath English Milk Chocolate Toffee Bits

1 tablespoon confectioners' sugar

I throw this dessert together for my girls when it's just the three of us. They scarf it up, and believe me: They can be finicky! I hope your family likes it as much as mine does—even the picky eaters.

APPLES WITH
RAS EL HANOUT AND GRANOLA

Preheat the oven to 300°F.

In a large mixing bowl, stir together the oats, walnuts, honey, and cinnamon. Spread the granola mixture evenly on a nonstick baking sheet and bake until lightly browned, 12 to 15 minutes. Stir the granola once or twice during baking to prevent sticking.

Remove the baking sheet from the oven and set the granola aside to cool.

In a bowl, whisk together the yogurt, cream, and confectioners' sugar until the sugar dissolves. Pour the mixture into a whipped cream siphon and screw 2 N_2O chargers in place, shaking the siphon well between each one. Set aside at room temperature until serving.

Scoop the apples into balls using a Parisian scoop or melon baller. Transfer to a bowl and sprinkle with the lemon juice. Add the granulated sugar and *ras el hanout* and toss well.

Set a large skillet over medium-high heat and, when hot, put the butter in the pan and let it melt. When the butter starts to foam, add the apples and cook until softened, 3 to 4 minutes.

Divide the apples among serving bowls and top with the granola. Using the siphon, top each serving with some of the yogurt mixture.

———

Note: Ras el hanout is a North African spice mixture that includes warm, aromatic spices such as cinnamon, ginger, allspice, and cumin. It's available in gourmet stores, Moroccan and other North African markets, and online.

SERVES 5

3 cups old-fashioned rolled oats

1 cup chopped walnuts

½ cup honey

1 teaspoon ground cinnamon

2 cups vanilla yogurt

½ cup heavy cream

2 tablespoons confectioners' sugar

3 apples, peeled and cored

Juice of 1 lemon

½ cup granulated sugar

3 tablespoons *ras el hanout* spice (see Note)

2 tablespoons unsalted butter

I make this with my kids all the time. It only takes minutes, and they love it. Be a good parent and make it for your kids, too, okay?

QUICK APPLE TARTS
WITH POTPOURRI SPICES

SERVES 4

4 tart apples, peeled, cored, and cut into thick wedges

2 tablespoons sugar

5 tablespoons unsalted butter, melted (I use clarified butter)

1 tablespoon *ras el hanout* spice (a North African spice blend), or apple pie spice

About 1 cup plain granola (your favorite)

Vanilla ice cream or sweetened whipped cream, for serving

Preheat the oven to 350°F.

In a large mixing bowl, toss the apples with the sugar.

In a large sauté pan, heat 2 tablespoons of the butter over medium-high heat. Add the apples and cook, stirring occasionally, until the apples begin to soften, about 2 minutes. Sprinkle the apples with the spices and cook until the apples are fragrant and a little softer, 3 to 4 minutes longer. Remove the pan from the heat and let the apples cool a little.

In a food processor fitted with the metal blade, pulse the granola with the remaining 3 tablespoons butter.

Divide the granola evenly among four 8-ounce ramekins or custard cups and press it firmly into the dishes. Bake for about 10 minutes to set the granola. Remove the ramekins from the oven and divide the apples among them, packing them gently on top of the granola.

Bake the apple tarts for about 15 minutes longer, or until they're bubbling hot. Serve with ice cream.

There's something deep in my soul that's triggered by the pairing of those two words: *banana* and *split*. Could be because of some deep, hidden childhood memory of going to the ice cream parlor with my grandmum, or maybe it's the audacious gluttony of the creation. Regardless, I'm obsessed.

The perfect banana split sports multiple kinds of ice cream and toppings of assorted flavors, textures, and temperatures that come together in what I consider a perfect dessert. Here's my slightly unorthodox, out-of-this-world, and super oversized version. Grab a spoon.

BLAIS BANANA SPLIT

Preheat the oven to 350°F. Line a shallow baking pan with aluminum foil or lightly spray it with flavorless vegetable oil.

Split the bananas in half lengthwise and arrange them, cut side up, in the baking pan. Drizzle with the honey and sprinkle with the granulated sugar and cinnamon so that they are nicely covered.

Bake the bananas for 12 to 15 minutes, until they soften and the honey coating is hot and liquidy.

In the chilled bowl of an electric mixer fitted with the whisk attachment or using a handheld electric mixer, beat the cream on medium-high speed until thick. Continue to beat while adding the confectioners' sugar until the cream forms soft, luxuriant peaks, 2 to 3 minutes. Set aside.

On a large platter, arrange the split bananas to form 4 slightly separate pairs with the inside edges touching; do your best; this doesn't have to be perfect. Top the 4 pairs of bananas with a scoop of each kind of ice cream so that there are 3 scoops on each banana. Drizzle the chocolate sauce over a scoop of ice cream on each pair of bananas, followed by the strawberry sauce and then the caramel sauce on the other scoops. Each scoop should have its own kind of sauce. (Alternatively, you can make 4 separate banana splits by putting a whole banana in each of 4 banana split dishes and proceeding with the recipe.)

Top the scoops of ice cream with dollops of whipped cream and then crown each banana split with nuts and 3 cherries. Serve immediately (as if you need to be reminded!).

SERVES 4

4 ripe but firm bananas

About ¼ cup honey

2 teaspoons granulated sugar

About 1 teaspoon ground cinnamon

1 cup cold heavy cream

1 tablespoon confectioners' sugar

4 scoops Marshmallow Ice Cream (page 237)

4 scoops Nutella Ice Cream (page 240)

4 scoops Amaretti Ice Cream (page 244)

½ cup Chocolate Sauce (page 246)

½ cup Strawberry Balsamic Sauce (page 247)

½ cup Miso-Caramel Sauce (page 245)

About ½ cup chopped walnuts or pecans

12 maraschino cherries, with stems

C'mon, you knew marshmallows would find further glory, even beyond s'mores! Once you try this ridiculously indulgent ice cream, you'll forget that graham crackers and chocolate bars even exist.

MARSHMALLOW
ICE CREAM

**MAKES ABOUT
1 QUART**

One 16-ounce bag marshmallows

1½ cups heavy cream

1½ cups whole milk

¾ cup sugar

2 teaspoons pure vanilla extract

About ½ cup Miso-Caramel Sauce (page 245) (optional)

Preheat the oven to 300°F.

Spread the marshmallows on a baking sheet and toast in the oven for 5 to 6 minutes, until lightly browned, turning them a few times to brown on all sides.

In a large saucepan, combine the cream, milk, sugar, and vanilla and heat over medium heat, stirring, until the sugar dissolves and the mixture is hot but not boiling.

Transfer the milk mixture to a blender, add the marshmallows, and blend until smooth. Pour the mixture into a bowl and cover it tightly with plastic wrap. Submerge the bowl in a larger bowl filled with cold water and ice and transfer both to the refrigerator to chill for at least 4 hours and up to 12 or overnight.

Transfer the chilled mixture to an ice cream maker and follow the manufacturer's instructions. When frozen (the ice cream will still be soft), transfer to a container with a tight-fitting lid and freeze until firm, at least 3 hours or up to 1 week.

Serve the ice cream with the Miso-Caramel Sauce drizzled over it, if using.

If you haven't been introduced to Nutella yet, a chocolate-hazelnut spread, what are you waiting for? I go on an occasional Nutella binge, which is nothing to be proud of. (I'm working on our relationship in therapy.) In the meantime, I came up with this seductive ice cream that is sinfully delicious on its own, or doused with chocolate sauce or caramel sauce—or both—or as part of a banana split.

NUTELLA ICE CREAM

MAKES ABOUT
1 QUART

1½ cups heavy cream

1 cup whole milk

½ cup sugar

5 large egg yolks

Kosher salt

1 cup Nutella

In a saucepan, combine 1 cup of the cream, the milk, and ¼ cup of the sugar and bring to a simmer over medium heat, stirring until the sugar dissolves.

In a heatproof mixing bowl, whisk the egg yolks with the remaining ½ cup cream and ¼ cup sugar until smooth. Gradually whisk ½ cup of the warm cream mixture into the egg mixture and, when smooth, pour the mixture into the saucepan.

Continue to cook, stirring constantly, until the custard is thick enough to coat the back of a wooden spoon (175°F on an instant-read thermometer), 10 to 15 minutes; do not let the custard boil or it will curdle!

Strain the custard mixture through a fine-mesh sieve into a bowl. Put this smaller bowl into a larger one partially filled with ice cubes and cold water. Stir occasionally until cool. Season with a pinch of salt and stir to mix.

Put the Nutella in the canister of blender and pour about 1 cup of the cooled custard into the blender. Pulse until smooth and then return to the bowl with the rest of the custard. Stir to mix.

Transfer the custard to an ice cream maker and freeze according to the manufacturer's instructions. When frozen (the ice cream will still be soft), transfer to a container with a tight-fitting lid and freeze until firm, at least 3 hours longer or up to 1 week.

Ice Cream Facts. No Fiction.

If you've ever made ice cream at home, you know how amazingly, incredibly, irresistibly delicious it is. But it's a production, no doubt about it, and it's so easy to buy. I mean, Ben & Jerry's is sold at those mini-marts attached to gas stations. Why bother with homemade?

I'll tell you why. Homemade ice cream is creamier, sweeter, and more indulgent than any other. I'm not saying commercial ice creams aren't good—they're great—but ice cream you make yourself falls into that category of foods that, for some enigmatic reason, just are better when made with your own two hands. Think homemade bread, homemade lemonade, homemade lasagna, homemade apple pie. Like these, homemade ice cream is head and shoulders above its commercial counterpart. And that's the way it is. The end.

To achieve the texture that only ice cream can claim, air has to be churned into the cream mixture during freezing. If you were to simply put a sweetened cream mixture in the freezer, you'd end up with a block of frozen cream. Not too appetizing.

In the old days, ice cream makers were hand cranked and required ice chips and salt to keep the inner canister cold. The salt prevented the ice from melting too quickly but occasionally seeped into the ice cream. Kinda yuk. These days you'll probably use an electric ice cream machine with a coolant-wrapped canister. No salt, no ice chips, but the canister must be frozen for hours and hours, until icy cold. And finally, after it's done and you scoop the ice cream from the canister, it won't be as firm as you expect. Transfer it to another container for further freezing—at least three hours longer, or until pleasingly firm. If you've room in your freezer, store the canister there so that you can make ice cream whenever you're inspired.

There are two kinds of ice cream: a custard-based version called French-style, and a simpler version made without eggs called Philadelphia-style or American-style. Hands down, custard-based ice creams are richer and, most say, better. They're a little harder to ace because you have to make custard and not let it curdle. (Not too hard, guys. Don't wig out.)

Finally, when you make ice cream, think cold. Cold, cold, cold metal bowls and utensils. Cold cream and cold milk. The custard is cooked, of course, but then it's chilled in an ice bath (a bowl filled with cold water and ice cubes) to bring its temperature way down before it's poured into the canister and churned into amazingly, incredibly, irresistibly delicious ice cream.

Trust the Italians to work the rich, mellow flavor of almonds into cookies and a liqueur—both of which I take full advantage of here.

AMARETTI
ICE CREAM

**MAKES ABOUT
1 QUART**

28 to 30 amaretti cookies

1½ cups whole milk

1½ cups heavy cream

½ cup sugar

¼ cup amaretto

4 large egg yolks

Kosher salt

Using your fingers, crumble the cookies into small uneven crumbs. You should have about ½ cup crumbs.

In a saucepan, combine the milk, 1 cup of the cream, and ¼ cup of the sugar and bring to a simmer over medium heat, stirring until the sugar dissolves. Stir in the amaretto.

In a heatproof mixing bowl, whisk the egg yolks with the remaining ½ cup cream and ¼ cup sugar until smooth. Gradually whisk ½ cup of the warm cream mixture into the egg mixture and, when smooth, pour the mixture into the saucepan.

Continue to cook, stirring constantly, until the custard is thick enough to coat the back of a wooden spoon (175°F on an instant-read thermometer), 10 to 15 minutes; do not let the custard boil or it will curdle!

Strain the custard mixture through a fine-mesh sieve into a bowl. Put this smaller bowl into a larger one partially filled with ice cubes and cold water. Stir occasionally until cool. Season with a pinch of salt and stir to mix.

Transfer the custard to an ice cream maker and freeze according to the manufacturer's instructions. When nearly frozen and the ice cream is thick, add the cookie crumbs. Continue to churn the ice cream. When frozen (the ice cream will still be soft), transfer to a container with a tight-fitting lid and freeze until firm, at least 3 hours longer or up to 1 week.

Take my word for it—this miso-spiked riff on salted caramel is better than salted caramel.

MISO-CARAMEL
SAUCE

In a saucepan, combine the cream, sugar, and vanilla and heat over medium heat, stirring, until the sugar dissolves. Add the miso and baking soda and cook until the liquid turns dark caramel, about 15 minutes longer, taking care to not let it burn.

Start adding the butter, a piece or two at a time. Stir the sauce as the butter is absorbed and don't add more until the previous pieces are incorporated. When it's done, the sauce will be satiny and buttery.

Use right away, or cool, cover, and refrigerate for up to 1 week. Heat gently before using.

**MAKES ABOUT
1 QUART**

1 cup heavy cream

2 cups sugar

1 teaspoon pure vanilla extract

1 tablespoon white miso

1 tablespoon baking soda

¾ cup (1½ sticks) unsalted butter, cut into pieces

Get in the habit of making this weekly so it's always on hand. You never know when you'll want some molten chocolate at breakfast, lunch, snacktime, dinner, dessert, or midnight.

CHOCOLATE
SAUCE

Put the chocolate in a heatproof bowl and set aside.

In a saucepan, combine the corn syrup with ½ cup water and set over medium-high heat, whisking to mix. Add the sugar and cocoa, whisking until smooth and incorporated. Bring the sauce to a boil.

Pour the boiling syrup over the chopped chocolate and whisk until smooth and thoroughly blended.

Set aside to cool a little before using. The sauce can be stored in a lidded container in the refrigerator for up to 1 week. Warm gently before using.

MAKES ABOUT 1 CUP

8 ounces bittersweet or semisweet chocolate, chopped

½ cup corn syrup

1 cup sugar

¼ cup unsweetened cocoa powder

Use the sweetest, reddest strawberries and the best, syrupy-est balsamic vinegar you can find. A taste of heaven.

STRawBERRY
BALSAMIC SAUCE

Coarsely chop the berries and transfer to a large bowl. Sprinkle with the sugar and vinegar. Cover and set aside at room temperature for at least 1 hour but no longer than 4 hours.

Transfer to a serving bowl and, just before serving, season the berries with the pepper. Mash them slightly if you think it's needed.

The berries can be refrigerated with their juices in an airtight container for up to 2 weeks.

MAKES ABOUT 2 CUPS

2 pints fresh strawberries, hulled

¼ cup sugar

2 tablespoons balsamic vinegar

¼ teaspoon freshly ground black pepper

NDEX

Note: Page references in *italics* indicate photographs.